1²⁵

Indoor Beauty with Vines

Indoor Beauty with Vines

new and practical ways to grow house plants

by jack kramer

illustrations by michael valdez

 walker and company • new york

First published in the United States of America in 1977 by the Walker Publishing Company, Inc.

Published simultaneously in Canada by Fitzhenry & Whiteside, Limited, Toronto.

Printed in the United States of America.

Design by J.M. Wall

CONTENTS

Introduction:

flowers on the wall

Of all house plants, vines are probably the most overlooked and yet the easiest of plants to grow. And they can make you an instant gardener, because they grow rapidly once started. In a few months you can have a colorful wall of passion flowers or morning glories, delicate traceries of ivy or jasmine, hand-wrought pictures of leaf and flower wherever you want them—for dividers, screens, on walls, or you-name-it. Vines can do all this and more—well grown and well trained, they are outstanding and will delight you.

With all these attributes, why haven't we heard more about vines? Simply because in the melee of house plants, they have been overlooked. Yet these old favorites can do more as decorative accents in the home than can many other house plants. Further, they are usually inexpensive.

Growing vines—flowering, and foliage ones too—allows you to use your imagination as well as your hands. Training and grooming vines to specific situations makes this not only a gardening hobby but a craft as well. And if growing vines brings out the artist in you—why not?

There are large vines and small ones, some with large leaves, others with tiny ones. Plumbago with blue flowers is stunning, lantana a colorful delight, and the lovely cup-and-saucer vine is always beautiful. Leafy vines like philodendrons and others too numerous to mention are also part of the wall-flower hobby.

Here is a whole new world of plant busy-ness to keep your fingers moving and your imagination soaring. Dig in and enjoy this climbing world of plants. These wall flowers, believe me, will make your rooms dance with color and beauty.

Jack Kramer

1

1

tHE bEAUTifuL viNES

Whatever you call them—climbers or trailers, crawlers or creepers—vines are overlooked plants. Yet, if you have some house plants (and most people do), you are probably harboring a gem of a vine. Vines are—in the world of plants—perhaps the most beautiful and luxuriant subjects.

Most vines grow quickly, offer a wealth of color in cascading sheets of leaf and flower, and can serve a multitude of uses: look stunning on trellises, frame windowsills, hide unsightly wall cracks, provide privacy at a window, or decorate a ceiling. What other plant can do that? Vines are the workhorse of a decorative indoor garden, and they qualify as nature's drapery, adorning both your windows and your home. In fact, some vines grow so quickly that you may find yourself in a jungle and rue the day you read this book!

We are familiar with outdoor vines like morning glory, clematis, bougainvillea, and wisteria. But can you name one indoor vine? Look around your home. If you have a philodendron , you probably have a

vining plant, because most philodendrons are viners. The wax plant, with its handsome oval leaves and waxy beautiful flowers, is an indoor vine, as are the wandering Jew (tradescantia) and the familiar cissus, or grape ivy.

Why make such a fuss over the vining plants? It is simply because these plants can do so much for you indoors to make your greeneries come to life and glow with color. You must try them to appreciate their usefulness and their dramatic appearance.

Foliage Favorites

Let's let our eyes wander over the meandering greenery of the world of vines (in this book we consider trailers, crawlers, and pendant growers as vines) and look at some of the old-time favorites. The softwood vines classified as cissus, popularly known as kangaroo ivy and grape ivy, are the primary favorites because so many people grow them. These plants have heart-shaped scalloped

Bougainvillea

Morning Glory

4

Fatshedera lizei

leaves and grow with little care in shade or bright light. Mine cover the top shelves of my kitchen cupboards with greenery; the cupboards are not near windows, yet the plants still prosper.

Across the room from the cupboards are my tradescantias. I have four varieties: the yellow-and-green form, the vibrant red type, the plain-green wandering Jew, and my favorite, the little-leaved tradescantia, which is a cascade of tiny green leaves.

The string-of-hearts plant has never been a favorite of mine, but its shower of tiny, heart-shaped, delicately veined leaves makes it popular with many people. The leaves are spaced far apart—unusual for vines—and although perhaps somewhat of a curiosity, this odd plant has its uses.

Asparagus sprengeri, not really a vine but growing with pendant branches, is a mass of feathery green. This is an undemanding plant that almost takes care of itself (although I am always complimented for keeping my asparagus so lush).

Fatshedera, not well known but lovely, has large leaves and is a cross between a fatsia and an English ivy. This vinelike shrub can reach 6 feet in height, enough to decorate a window frame or serve as a screen.

My creeping fig (*Ficus pumila*), with its tiny and delicate heart-shaped leaves, originally started outdoors in my vestibule. By some quirk of nature it found a niche and invaded the indoors. This rampant grower now defiantly grows on a pane of glass inside, providing a tapestry of color that delights my eyes and guests' too. This particular plant climbs and clambers on stone or glass surfaces by means of suction disks. Creeping fig has saved me from curtaining the side windows so people cannot peer into the house.

Scindapsus, with green-and-gold leaves, and syngonium, with arrow-shaped leaves, are other less-known but equally attractive vines. And not to be overlooked are the many philodendrons. The philodendrons comprise a large group of mostly vining plants, some with solid leaves, some with deeply lobed leaves, but most with large, dark-green leaves. In nature, philodendrons grow on trees, wrapping their stems around branches and festooning the tree in glorious color. (No, philodendrons are not parasites; they merely use the tree as a host.) These plants will grab onto a piece of bark or a small trellis if you put it in the pot. Philodendrons are eager to grow and have a myriad of uses in the home; Chapter 7 includes a list of philodendrons you can grow indoors.

Philodendron

Flowering Gems

If you think vines are just foliage plants, open your eyes. Look at bougainvillea, which has bright red bracts (and is also a good indoor plant). Or consider the lipstick vine (aeschynanthus) or the often overlooked but stellar glory bower, technically known as clerodendrum—what a harvest of color in one plant!

Columneas, members of the gesneriad family, have bright orange or yellow flowers, and the amenable Mexican love vine (dipladenia) is a halo of bright pink color in a basket container. From June to October the love vine puts on its show for all to see, and a better flowering plant is hard to find.

The wax plant (*Hoya carnosa*) should probably be listed in the foliage class because most people cannot get it to bear flowers. But mature plants will bloom, and the flowers are so spectacular—bunches of waxy white, scented blooms—that the wax plant is definitely a flowering item.

Some jasmines, with white, scented flowers, do magnificently in the home. I have one in my living room doorway, where its evening scent delights people. If you are brave and courageous and want a challenge, try passion flowers. Just as pretty as a jasmine are plumbago, with blue flowers; thunbergia, the black-eyed Susan; and the exotic vanilla, an orchid with incredible yellow flowers that will stun the eye with their beauty. Unfortunately, vanilla is a most difficult plant; only once in 15 years have I coaxed mine into bloom. Yet the oval leathery green leaves are handsome, so vanilla grows in the plant room year after year. It is now 15 feet long and still a challenge to me.

These are only some of the foliage and flowering vines; Chapters 7 and 8 give complete plant lists, with descriptions.

2

how [and where] to use vines

I have never really indiscriminately grown plants. I feel that plants should serve a purpose: as decoration, as accent, as additional horizontal or vertical lines in a room, or as color accent. In all my books I stress *the use of plants*, because they are so versatile and can do so much to add charm and livability to a home. Vines are no exception; they can be used in a myriad of ways to help the home become a more cheerful and bright place.

There is absolutely nothing wrong and quite everything right with incorporating vines into a room divider or using vines at windows in place of curtains. Vines well trained on trellises make handsome wall pictures silhouetted against pastel-colored walls. If the architecture of your home allows it, vines can become delightful indoor post gardens.

Vines as Dividers

My kitchen and dining room are actually one large area, and I wanted definition between the areas when I remodeled the house. A wall was out of the question because each "room" was too small, and a wall would have only made the situation worse. So I installed a bookcase-shelf unit, which separated the two but allowed air and light into each area. Once in place, this unit was satisfactory but somewhat sterile, so I started putting plants at the ends of some shelves and all along one shelf. I added trellises for plants to grow on. This worked like magic—now I have a room divider that is functional as well as beautiful to look at. Small-leaved tradescantias provide a tracery of beauty, and the dark-green, bold color of the kangaroo ivy on the top shelf is a perfect contrast to the lighter green, smaller leaved tradescantias.

The beauty of the dividers is further enhanced by a lovely green-and-white zebrina growing up from a bottom shelf and invisibly tacked to the side walls of the divider shelf. To complete the handsome arrangement, a basket of lipstick vine hangs from the ceiling, with the container slightly above eye level in front of the shelves. The total result

Ficus pumila

is not a jungle as you might think, but almost a painted picture of greenery. I trim and remove the leaves of plants as necessary to keep the proportions and growth habits within bounds on all the plants.

Another idea for growing vines as dividers is to tack small pieces of wood (lath) in a trellis effect over a section of the divider or bookcase, as I did; this gives vines something to climb on and creates a tracery of green. (See Chapter 4.)

Vines as Wall Pictures

If I told you that you could grow vines on your walls, you would probably tell me I was carrying my point a bit too far. However, *Ficus pumila* and many of the philodendrons will do just that—grow on walls! This is hardly satisfactory for the walls, however, especially if you are renting, so you must devise a setup that will accomodate these reaching plants. Trellises can, of course, be placed in front of the walls (not attached to walls) and anchored in the planter boxes. This works fine, and we explore this facet of wall growing in Chapter 4.

You can also use a wall picture, a box and frame hung like a picture. The front of the picture box is covered with sphagnum moss and hardware cloth so plants have something to grow on. The effect of wall panels of plants is especially handsome in nooks and crannies; it creates a wall of green or can be used simply as a picture. It provides unique eye interest. One word of caution: do not get carried away and let the vine engulf the room (and this can happen). Keep it in bounds on the wall plaque. Trim and prune as necessary to keep a pattern going, so the wall tracery is always simple and attractive, never straggly and rampant. Do not make the wall pictures too large; make them a suitable size that you can handle easily. In Chapter 4 we show and tell you how to make these wall pictures.

Vines as Window Traceries

Large, empty windows invariably need decoration, and potted plants on sills in regimented rows is the usual answer. There is nothing wrong with this, but for a different effect try window traceries of plant leaves. Sometimes you can just set a plant in a corner of the window sill and allow it to climb with supporting devices like U-shaped wire holders. I saw a wax plant that ran the entire perimeter of a window, providing a charming effect.

If you want to be more subtle about the setup, make a string or wire trellis in the window. Place tacks at the bottom and top of the window and stretch wire or string on them in a handsome pattern. Start plants in pots at the base and train them to the trellis. The effect is as handsome as that of a string trellis against a wall.

You can also use two or three hanging baskets placed at varying levels (stairstep fashion) at the window. Support the plants from strong ceiling hooks. This form of green decoration has become very popular because the cascading plants create a fountain of color at the window and look good from both inside and outside.

Note that there is more to window decoration than just growing plants; a certain amount of artistic talent is necessary to create the handsome leaf patterns. You do not want too much, just enough to obscure the windows (and save drapery bills) and create some natural beauty indoors. Vines can do it!

Vines as Post Gardens

Not every apartment or home has posts, pillars, or other upright members, but many do, and even though these verticals can be left bare, often they require some decoration. Posts tend to develop cracks, so some camouflage is often in order. Gardens on posts are lovely outdoors, but they can be overpowering indoors. Use this mode of vine decoration with discretion.

To have post gardens, you must have something at the base of the posts for plants to grow in (this is covered in Chapter 3). The box or planter will house the vine; train the vine to the post with tie-ons, small wire clasps, or hardware devices. No matter what kind of planter you select, remember that it will be directly on the floor, which requires some form of stain protection. Use a metal insert inside the box to catch excess water, or place pots in saucers (although pots do not have the finished or custom look that boxes have). Also, install a cork pad under the planter or box to be doubly sure moisture evaporation does not mar wood surfaces or carpeting.

If you feel very energetic, you can even make your own post gardens—post and all—by using four very narrow trellises in a planter. This particular plant aid is quite handsome indoors, but it is not commercially available; it is something you will have to make. Done well, with painted trellises, a homemade post garden can be a stunning addition to a room.

3

Getting Plants Growing

To get plants growing you will need some containers. Most plants look fine in standard clay pots, but with vines you have to be more imaginative because they can grow very tall and tend to be rangy. Usually the small clay pot or larger tub is not in scale with the vining plants, but planters and boxes are perfect. A planter is a rectangular wooden or clay housing, usually long and narrow, ideal for vines growing on trellises. A box is usually 10, 16, or 20 inches square. Boxes and planters have more depth and visual mass to carry a large vine than a single round pot does.

There are commercially made planters and boxes available, but they only come in certain sizes, and often, when working with vines, you will want a box or planter to fit a specific area. Thus, you might want to make your own—and nothing beats the custom look!

Planters

Commercial planters are generally made of wood or clay. (There are also plastic ones, but they are not esthetically pleasing.) The clay planter has a simple elegance and looks good in almost any situation; the wood planter (usually redwood) is fine too and blends with most interiors. These planters are usually, but not always, sold at nurseries. Search for them, or watch garden ads. Avoid at all costs the red-stained planter box carried in suppliers' yards; the box just does not look good and invariably falls apart in a short time.

If you make your own planters (and I strongly advise this, because it is cheaper and the planter will be better looking), use kiln-dried, finished redwood or cedar if you want to leave the outside natural. If you are going to paint the planter box to match existing color schemes, pine or fir will do fine. (The box painted in shiny enamel has a very handsome look; I prefer to paint my containers.) You can also have boxes custom made by a carpenter. This is more expensive but not exorbitant.

With any planter or box, whether purchased or custom made, always be sure there are drain holes in the bottom. All planters and boxes will need some type of drip tray to catch

13

POLISHED SHEET ALUMINUM COVERING

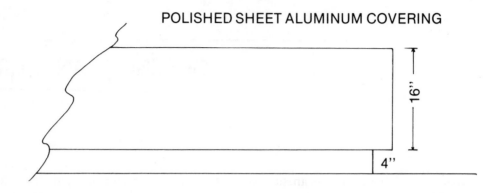

16"

4"

GRAVEL IN ALUMINUM PAN

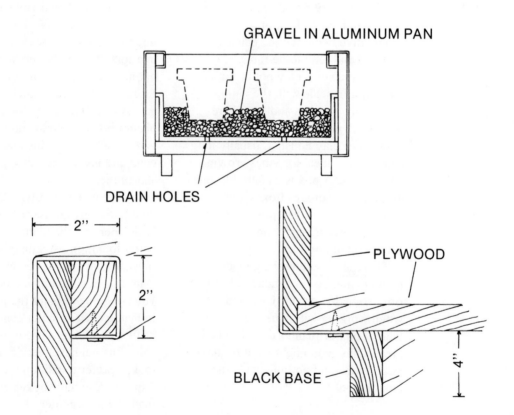

DRAIN HOLES

2"

2"

PLYWOOD

4"

BLACK BASE

PLANTER BOX DETAILS

excess water. But drip trays are not available commercially. For years I have been using cookie sheets or other kitchen baking pans, but they do leave something to be desired in looks. A better solution, and one I strongly recommend if you have the extra money, is to have custom trays 1-inch deep made by a sheet-metal house. Then planter, plant, and tray will look like a handsome, total unit.

Occasionally you might find some shallow plastic trays you can use to catch excess water. These come in colors—the more neutral the color, the better the looks.

Clay Pots

The standard terra cotta pot has been used for years and is an ideal container for most plants. Unfortunately, terra cotta pots look out of scale with a sprawling vine; this is not a serious objection, but it does bear some consideration if you are really design oriented. To rectify this problem, use good-looking trellises that are substantial and sturdy, to offset the proportions of plant and pot. (I discuss trellises fully in Chapter 4.)

Another solution I have used successfully, and one you can try (it is inexpensive), involves five 6-inch pots placed in a row; this furnishes the needed horizontal mass. For vertical proportion, insert a $\frac{1}{2} \times \frac{1}{2}$-inch piece of wood 3 to 4 feet high in each pot. Put cross members of wood in place (or tie a string across) to create one "pot" out of five, or so it will seem.

Still another idea that works for me is to use a very low terra cotta pot, approximately five inches high and fourteen to eighteen inches in diameter. Staple together a piece of hardware cloth so that it forms a cylinder; place the cylinder into the soil (plants should already be in the soil). It takes some doing to really anchor the base of the hardware-cloth cylinder into the soil, so insert it deeply to make sure it stays upright. Now cautiously and carefully pull stems through the openings in the hardware cloth to start training them to climb. This takes patience—but so does watching soap operas, yet people do it.

Use a hardware or wire cloth that has $\frac{1}{2}$- to 1-inch openings between wires. Wire cloth is available at hardware stores; it is usually sold for screens or as fence material, depending upon its size. Use your imagination, but be smart: wear gloves. You wrap the cylinder together and staple it up and down to make it stay as a cylinder and not snap back at you. This is not easy, either, because wire has a mind of its own, but the procedure is not dangerous. The wire cylinder of vines makes a unique accent in any room, and the circle of color is indeed handsome. People ask me how in the world I managed it; my reply is always, "With care."

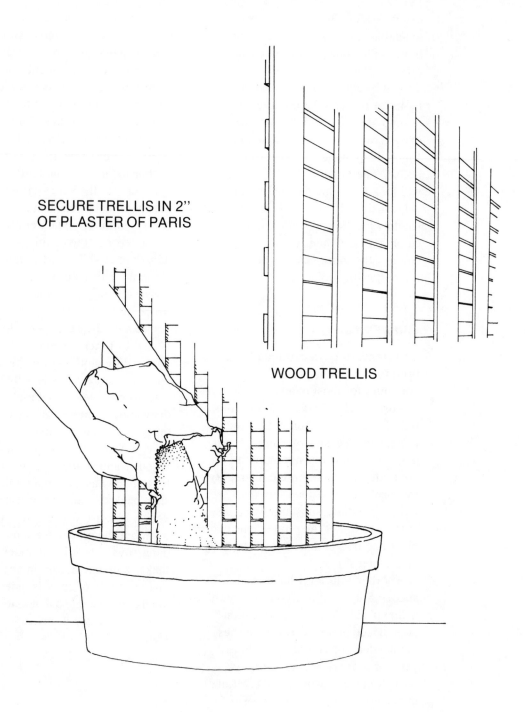

SECURE TRELLIS IN 2"
OF PLASTER OF PARIS

WOOD TRELLIS

TRELLIS IN POT

ROLL HARDWARE CLOTH
INTO 4" COLUMN

ADD SOIL
IN SMALL AMOUNTS

APROX. 14"

1"

4"

PLANT VINES AS
COLUMN IS FILLED
TO THE LEVEL OF EACH
HOLE IN THE MESH

SECURE IN CONTAINER
WITH PLASTER

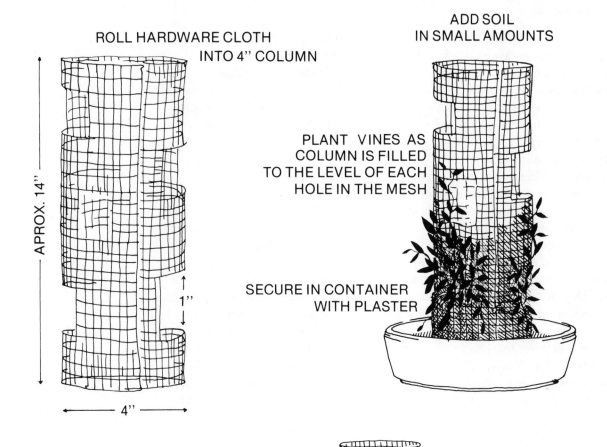

HAIR PIN SPHAGNUM MOSS OVER
EXPOSED SOIL AND MESH

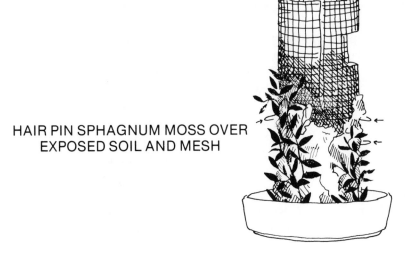

WIRE CYLINDER

Hardware and Attaching Devices

When you are working with vines you must also work with devices that keep vines attached to supports. When I was a kid I used adhesive tape to stick vines to walls and ceilings. But today manufacturers make many types of attaching devices, including standard vine clamps. However, the clamps are really best for outdoor work. The best tie device for indoor vines seems to be good old string or a commercial product called Tie-ems, which is a light, plastic, green tape that comes in a roll and is not objectional to the eye. Do not worry too much about the appearance of string and plastic tie-ons, because in a short time foliage will cover them.

Certainly not hardware, and not even an attaching device, is the natural vining supports that plants have. As we briefly mentioned in Chapter 1, Mother Nature has equipped her plants with many ingenious devices to hold onto objects as the vines crawl and creep. Some vines, like *Ficus pumila*, have suction disks, other vines have tendrils that wrap around wood supports, and philodendrons send out aerial roots that wrap around almost any surface after a while. All you really need to do is give nature a helping hand. Get the vine started on its host with tie-ons or string, and eventually the vine will do its own thing with dexterity.

I had a morning glory growing on a white trellis in the plant room—what color! I never got around to attaching the morning glory to the wood support, but I was amazed to discover that it did its own attaching. Don't tell me plants are not alive! This one literally wrapped itself around the trellis, in and out, with amazing speed—a real self-starter. In fact, the morning glory is so keen to live that when the plant finally died—it is grown for only a season indoors—I had a very difficult time extricating it from the wood trellis. The strength of this vine is astonishing.

It is trailing plants like chlorophytum and cissus, which do not have natural self- adhering devices, that you will have to devote training time to. Trailing plants are pendant growers, not really climbers, so you will have to help them along if you want them to grow vertically.

Helpful Hints

Most vines growing upright will continue to do so, and eventually the base of the plant may become somewhat bare. This is merely a hazard of growing vines. But what to do? Simply plant some small plants at the base to cover the nakedness.

Trailers also have a problem. After a time the plant becomes top- or bottom-heavy, and leaves and branches either die or snap off at the base. To prevent this, carefully cut and trim stems (as discussed in Chapter 6).

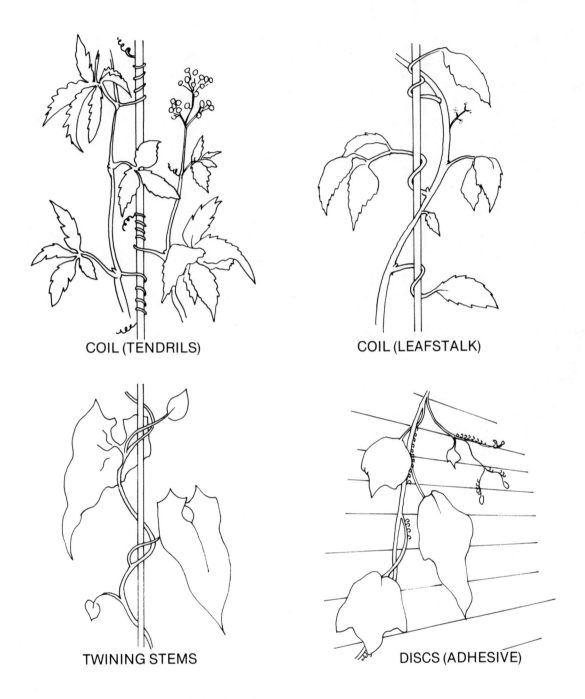

COIL (TENDRILS)

COIL (LEAFSTALK)

TWINING STEMS

DISCS (ADHESIVE)

HOW VINES CLING

fRAMES ANd suppORTS

All the beauty you get from vines does not come without some work on your part. True, for the most part vines will, with sufficient water and light, grow and grow and grow. But you must pitch in and help plants a little, which means supplying the frames and supports vines need to grasp.

Trellises are now very popular, as they were in Victorian times, and they do have a charm of their own. Making a trellis is not really that difficult—once you have the wood. Then it is a matter of tacking and gluing. By the way, we stress wood for trellises, but rope, string, and wire work equally well.

Dividers are really furniture and probably should not be included here. But because they are not that difficult to make, we include some drawings for constructing them. Of course, you can always buy your own dividers, in the form of book shelves and such.

Other miscellaneous supports and frames will also be discussed here, to get your imagination going and your vines growing. It is all fun and original and allows you to use your imagination.

Trellises

A trellis is a wood support, usually made with strips of wood crisscrossed to form a grid, diamond, or starburst pattern. The trellis has two stakes at its bottom; the stakes are inserted into the soil of the container to keep the trellis upright. You can make trellises from strips of wood, or buy commercial ones. The container trellis is not easy to find at suppliers, but the outdoor trellis is usually sold at most places. Some of the smaller outdoor trellises can be converted into pot trellises, but generally, making your own trellises is the best solution. Cost is minimal, and if you are at all handy with a hammer and nails, construction is easy. The size and construction of the trellis will depend on the pot and plant. Small trellises are fine for pots, but larger trellises are necessary for planters.

Redwood is the best wood to use, but cedar or pine is fine if you want to paint the trellis. No matter which wood you use, buy lumber cut to size (it is a little more expensive, but worth it). Then all you have to do is tack or glue the wood into suitable patterns.

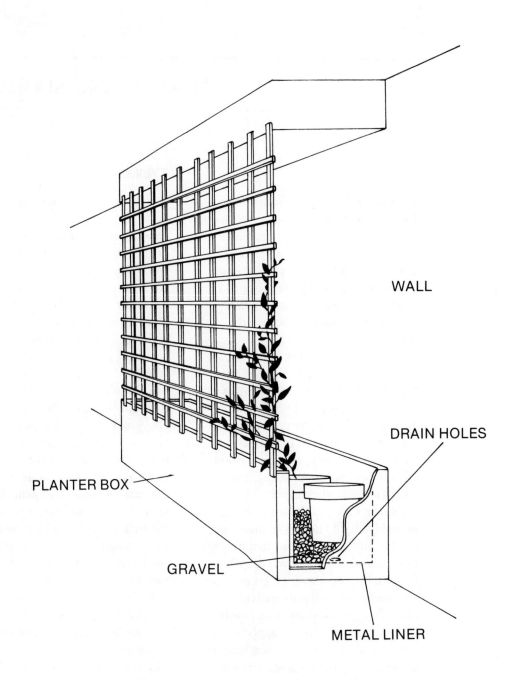

WALL

DRAIN HOLES

PLANTER BOX

GRAVEL

METAL LINER

TRELLIS DIVIDER

For large areas where a single tub or pot would not do, use long wooden or clay planters and erect suitable square or rectangular trellises. In such a situation the trellis has to be sturdily built with 1 × 1s for a frame and 1 × ½-inch wood strips for the patternwork.

Screens and Dividers

Usually a screen or divider is a shelf unit or a bookcase. Vines add great beauty to these pieces of furniture because they soften the lines of otherwise square, sterile furniture, and they also add color. Buy your divider or screen, or make your own if you are handy with tools.

Another attractive screen effect, and one I used in Chicago to cover an ugly corner radiator, is a trellis screen made from string. I spaced small nails (you could also use screw eyes) every 12 inches in the floor and directly above in the ceiling. Then I strung nylon string in simple parallel lines up and down across the 5-foot corner area. At the bottom I used metal planter bins and started growing *Philodendron hastatum* up the strings. I used two planter boxes with six plants, three plants to a box. In about three months—after the plants were trained—I had a lovely green screen that certainly covered the hideous heating element.

Window Tapestries

Using the same principle as the string trellis, you can have leafy plants at windows, as substitutes for curtains.

Small-leaved plants like *Ficus pumila* or grape ivy work well to create a tapestry effect. Place round-headed tacks at the edge of the windowsill and above in the top frame. You can vary the string design to make a diamond pattern, or just use parallel lines. Put small planter boxes on the sills behind the string trellis, and train plants up the string to create an unusual effect. Again, small-leaved vines work best to create a delicate, pretty picture.

When you use screens and windows of foliage, you must trim and cut off leaves frequently. You want to create a pattern of leaves, not a jungle that shuts out all light from the window. You can be quite artistic and train plants to specific patterns and create an effective "drapery." The cost is minimal, way below what you would pay for draperies. Of course this effect would not be suitable for all rooms, but it does work well in most situations, especially at kitchen windows.

Wall Gardens

There is absolutely nothing wrong with flowers on the wall—in this case, living plants. These unusual wall gardens add a great flair to a room. More importantly, they provide color, form, and accent, and if you care to call them plant sculptures, that's fine, too.

Just where you put your vertical living garden is important; select a place where it will be on display, where it will receive sufficient natural light, and where some water on the

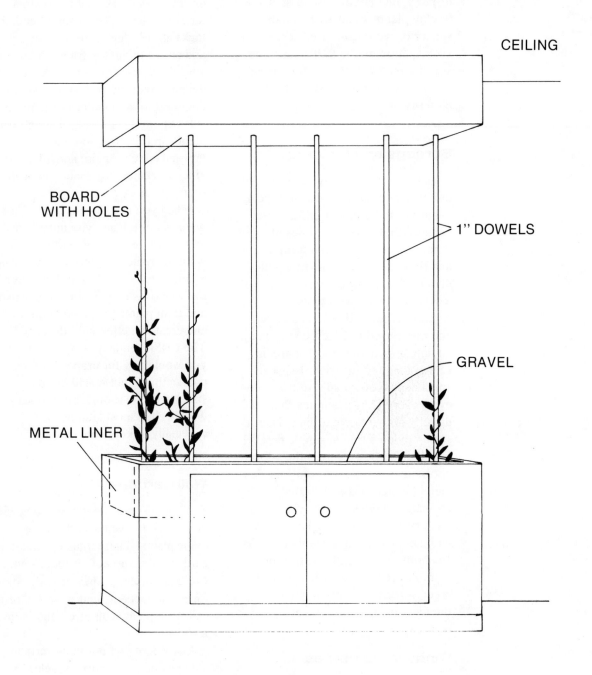

CEILING

BOARD
WITH HOLES

1" DOWELS

GRAVEL

METAL LINER

POLE DIVIDER

24

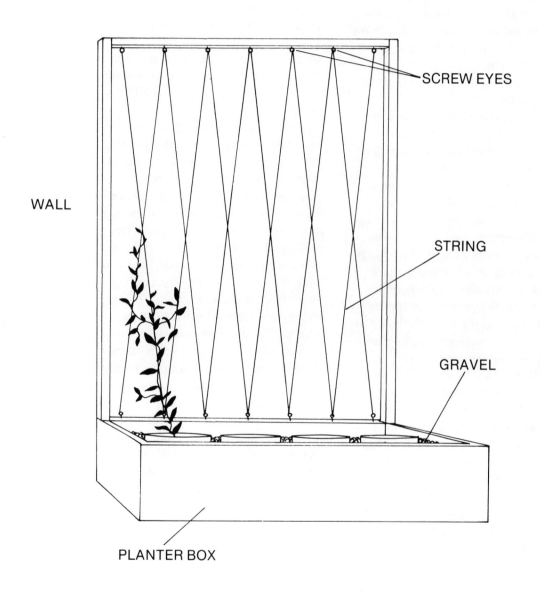

SCREW EYES

WALL

STRING

GRAVEL

PLANTER BOX

STRING SCREEN

floor (a few drops now and then) will not be objectionable. I recently saw a lovely wall garden in a small alcove of an apartment, where the floor was tile. A large vine provided beautiful contrast to the room.

No matter where the wall garden is, you will need a suitable planter (or a large clay pot) to hold soil at the base. The vine is started in the planter and travels the length of the wall plaque.

To make this vertical tracery, first select a suitable board (exterior plywood) and frame; you can make your own or buy ready-made ones at a frame shop. Apply a 1- to 2-inch bed of osmunda to the board with wires. (Osmunda is available at orchid suppliers, and wire at hardware stores.) Use a heavy gauge wire to keep the osmunda in place; direct contact against the board is necessary. When you have applied the wire (wrap it around the board as you would around a package), then get a sheet of hardware cloth (available at hardware stores). Staple this to the board, stapling around the perimeter so the bed of osmunda is securely fastened. Place the wall garden a few inches above the planter or pot; secure it to the wall as you would a picture.

Once the vines start growing, give them a helping hand; set them in place against the wire cloth; tie them or, in some cases, many vines will find their own way. You can grow almost any type plant on the wall garden to create this distinctive piece.

Totem Pole Magic

If you have seen a philodendron in a florist shop, you have probably seen a "totem pole." This is a wooden support, usually pressed tree-fern fiber, used in pots to support vining philodendrons. Actually, there is little wrong with this pole idea, but there is nothing great about it either; it looks like a square stick coming out of the pot and will always look like a square stick.

True, plants grow well on moistened poles and readily attach themselves to it, but what do you do when the plant reaches the top and has nowhere to go? Getting another pole—a taller one—to replace the original does not work, because you will murder the plant if you try to pull it loose from its original host. Do you glue the taller pole onto the existing one? No! So be forewarned: Totem poles have their uses, but their use stops at about 4 feet, and some vines can clamber to 15 feet, even indoors. Not a complete solution to the totem pole problem, but one that looks better, is a simple chunk of hollowed-out wood or bark of a tree. Look around your neighboring tree areas to find such a piece of wood and give it a try as a totem pole.

STAPLE HARDWARE CLOTH OVER
SPHAGNUM ONTO 24'' X 36'' PLYWOOD
BOARD

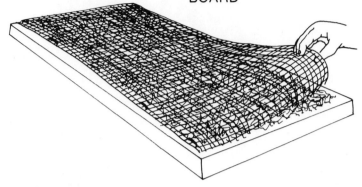

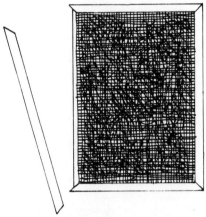

SECURE PLANT ROOTS INTO MOSS

ASSEMBLE AND ATTACH REDWOOD
FRAMES TO PLYWOOD BOARD

WATER BY SPRAYING

WALL PANEL

5

ESPALIER

The art of growing plants against a flat surface—a trellis or wall—is known as espalier. Centuries ago it was a common practice to grow fruit trees in this manner to save space and to give them protection from weather.

While it is not feasible to grow fruit trees indoors in this manner, there are some bushy plants that are handsome when grown in the espalier pattern. These plants—plumbago, *Euphorbia splendens*, and others—make a distinctive pattern and afford a unique accent in the home when grown on trellis screens or dividers. (In Chapters 7 and 8 we look at some that are suitable to this kind of gardening.)

Espaliers, be forewarned, do need attention; plants must be trained and pruned throughout the year. Still, the effort is worth the time, because of the unusual and pretty results.

Where to Use Espalier

The distinctive patterns of espalier make it especially suitable for home decoration. Somewhat like a painting or a tapestry, depending on which pattern you choose, espalier can be used in various ways to add beauty indoors.

A simple espalier pattern on a trellis against a window can create a dazzling effect and substitute for drapery; it affords a privacy factor while still allowing light to enter a room. The espalier against a window can be done by growing plants in separate pots; arrange a row of pots at the base of the window and train the vines to a pattern. Of course, a planter box could also be used as a container for the plants.

As a divider, espaliered plants are very satisfactory because they eliminate the need of a screen between, say, the dining room and kitchen and at the same time they provide a cheerful and colorful note to the area. The espalier is, of course, much more unusual than a simple divider. And it will generally cost much less money than the piece of furniture or bookcase so often used in these areas.

When used as a divider or window decoration, the espalier must be

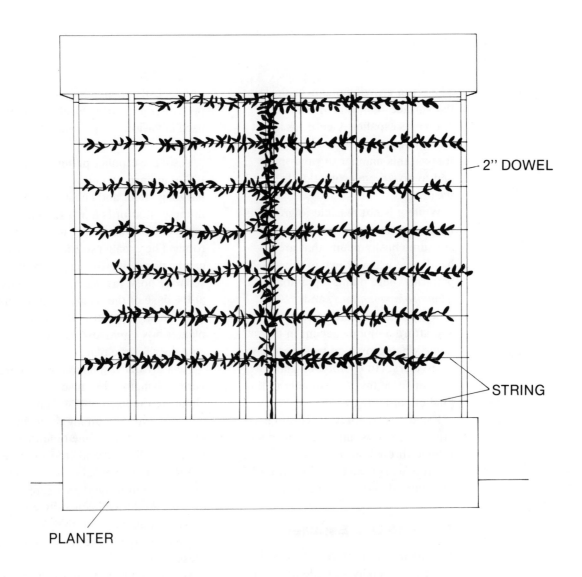

2" DOWEL

STRING

PLANTER

DIVIDER (HORIZONTAL "T")

correctly proportioned. For dividing a room area, the espalier is usually made the size of a standard divider (6 feet tall), and in windows it extends to the top of the window sash. However, an espalier can also be a ceiling-to-floor panel; in this case it becomes the accent of the room and as such is as lovely as a handsome painting or tapestry. A cascading wall of green is stunning.

Patterns

Years ago there were rigid espalier patterns—a vertical U shape, a horizontal T, or a double horizontal cordon, for example. The patterns were formal and symmetrical, to be used in outdoor gardens for their decorative effect. Today the patterns are more informal and thus more natural, and there are no rigid patterns you must follow when espaliering a plant. So we are using the word *espalier*, but it has a different meaning to us today. Basically, when you espalier a plant you are creating a pattern—any pattern—by removing some branches, some leaves, and more or less daylighting the plant—that is, leaving plenty of space between branches so the negative area becomes the pattern.

Because some guideline is needed, let's look at the old-fashioned patterns, and then you can borrow from them:

The double horizontal cordon. A center shoot about 20 inches high with two horizontal branches in each direction. Needs lots of space.

The vertical U shape. A vertical stem on each side of a central trunk.

The palmette verrier. A handsome candelabra pattern.

The palmette oblique. Branches trained in a fan shape.

Belgian espalier. A diamond pattern. Lovely.

Arcure. A series of connecting arcs.

As mentioned above it would be difficult to maintain these patterns indoors. But you can certainly borrow from them to create your own individual wall-plant patterns.

How to Do It

Use a strong trellis for the wall plants, and be sure it is securely fastened in the planter box. Use 2 × 4s for a frame, with a center brace (a 2 × 4) placed vertically in the center. Make a trellis pattern that has enough space between the wood laths or strips so that you can easily fasten stems to the wood with tie-ons. A simple 2-inch grid pattern works well. Don't make the trellis too large—a maximum size would be 48 inches (dividers are usually this width).

In Chapter 4 we talked about frames and supports, and you can follow plans and drawings in that chapter to build your espalier trellis. It is not easy, but it is not too difficult, either, and since plants look so good trained to pattern this is a worthwhile project for the adventurer.

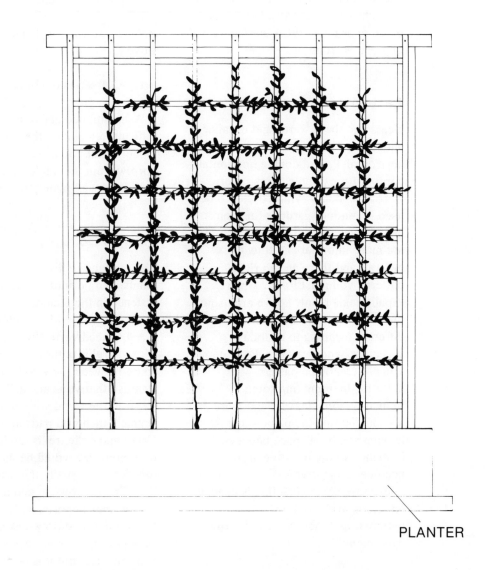

PLANTER

AGAINST WINDOW (GRID)

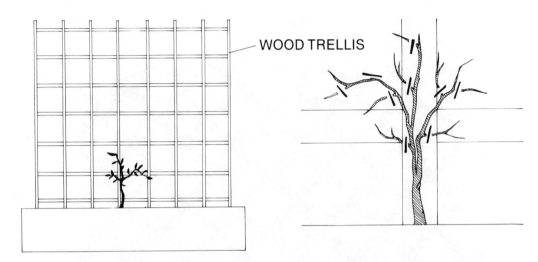

WOOD TRELLIS

ONE MAIN SPROUT IN CENTER OF GRID

CUT OFF ALL SIDE SHOOTS, LEAVING 3 HEADERS

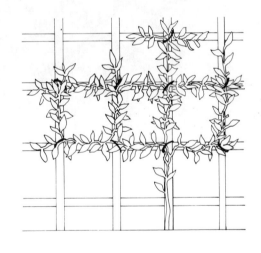

GUIDE BRANCHES BY TYING TO TRELLIS WITH STRING

CONTINUE TRIMMING SIDE SHOOTS WHILE TRAINING

TRAINING ESPALIERS (GRID)

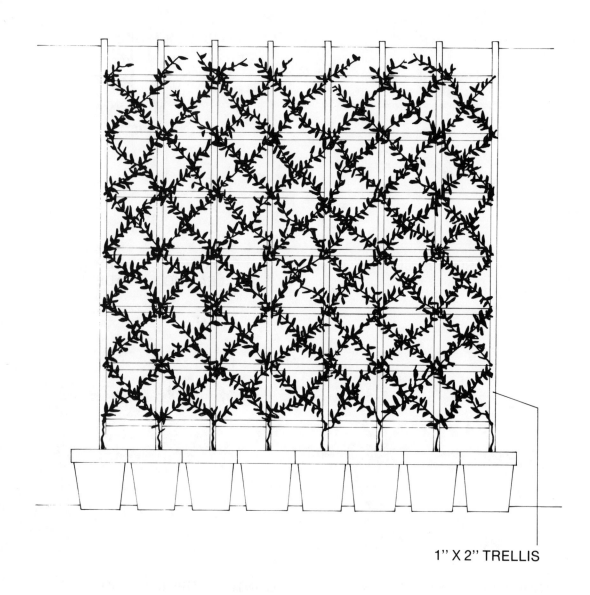

1'' X 2'' TRELLIS

CEILING TO FLOOR (DIAMOND)

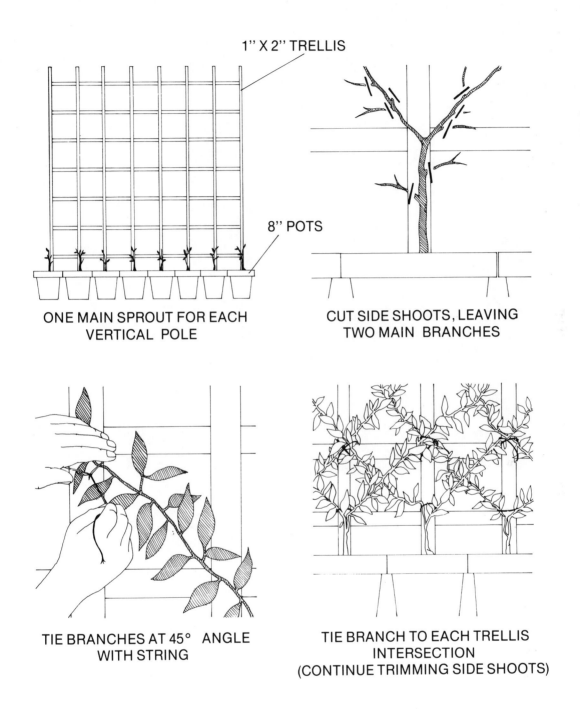

1" X 2" TRELLIS

8" POTS

ONE MAIN SPROUT FOR EACH
VERTICAL POLE

CUT SIDE SHOOTS, LEAVING
TWO MAIN BRANCHES

TIE BRANCHES AT 45° ANGLE
WITH STRING

TIE BRANCH TO EACH TRELLIS
INTERSECTION
(CONTINUE TRIMMING SIDE SHOOTS)

TRAINING ESPALIERS (DIAMOND)

6

TRAiNiNG ANd GROOMiNG YOUR plANTS

Most house-plant books do not
include a section on training and
grooming plants, but in a book about
vining and climbing plants it is
essential to have this information.
You will be working with plants that
take up lots of space, so you must
know how to keep them within
bounds. And this is not done by
simply ripping off leaves or stems.
There is a definite art to training
plants to trellises or supports, which
is what this chapter is about.

If you are not willing to work with
your vining plants and use your
imagination to make specific growing
patterns for them, stick to upright
standard growers. The viners need
help from you to be at their best
indoors, so be prepared. You will
find that it is a great deal of fun to use
your fingers and skill to fashion
plants into beautiful pictures and
patterns.

Plants' Growing Habits

Trailing or cascading plants like
chlorophytum and Swedish ivy by
nature grow pendant, with several

stems and many leaves to a stem.
This creates a lush look but also
eventually becomes a tangled mass.
With plants of this kind you have to
remove some leaves to give other
leaves space to expand in and to
provide for good air circulation. It
may seem cruel to cut off leaves
randomly, but it is necessary with
plants of this type, to keep them
looking their best. How many leaves
do you cut? When? Generally, plants
have a specific leaf pattern: two
leaves from one side of the stem, two
from the other, and so on. It is time
to do some cosmetic surgery when
the leaves become so crowded on the
stems and so overlapping that they
exclude air. Never remove too many
leaves—this takes too much strength
from the plant. Removing, say, three
to six leaves on a 12- to 18-inch stem
will hurt nothing and in fact, makes
for a healthier plant. Do this pruning
in the spring.

To avoid the common top-heavy
look many trailing plants have, allow
six or seven stout stems rather than a
dozen or more to develop per 8-inch
pot. This will also prevent stem bend

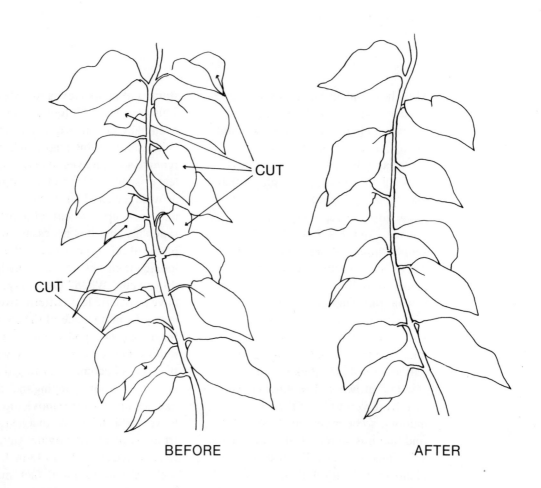

CUT

CUT

BEFORE

AFTER

PRUNING VINE (FOLIAGE)

at the rim of the plant, a very common malfunction of trailing plants.

Each individual plant requires specific cutting. For example, you would not cut a morning glory or a Christmas cactus because both plants naturally grow with sparse foliage, but you would cut plants like philodendrons, Swedish ivy, and tradescantias.

The vining plants (true viners) have more or less worked out their own system of leaf growth, and Mother Nature takes care of spacing in these plants. Most vines do not have an excess of leaves on their stems. True viners usually have one leaf or a pair of leaves on each side of a stem, with space between each leaf-growth segment. Viners require more tying to a support rather than cutting. However, they do occasionally need some stem surgery so that several stout stems rather than many weak ones will grow.

When you start to cut leaves or stems, first look at the plant from a distance rather than close up. Take a leaf off here or there; back up and observe again before you do more cutting. Trimming an indoor plant is the same as pruning an outdoor tree: you want to "daylight" the plant; that is, let air (and light) enter the center of the plant so good growth can continue.

Cutting and Trimming

The only tools you need for removing leaves and stems of plants are small hand pruning shears, small manicure scissors, and a small pocket knife.

When you remove a leaf from a stem, do it with one clean sharp cut and cut as close to the stem as possible. Always use clean, sterile tools; I sterilize my scissors and knife by running them through a flame. After making the cut, dust some powdered charcoal on the wound to seal it and prevent any infection from entering the area. When you cut stems, cut them about 1 inch above the soil line, not down into the soil. Again, infection may enter, so leave 1 inch of stem, and dust the cut with charcoal so that it callouses and hardens to form a scar.

Whenever you have done some cutting, try to avoid getting water on the plant afterward for a day or so. Water splashes, and it can get into open cuts and help cause rot, which you want to avoid. Even with charcoal on wounds, it takes a day or more for sap to stop running and cuts to heal.

Trimming plants means paring off decayed, yellow, or dried parts of leaves. Trimming involves shaping the leaf after you have removed the injured part and is necessary, if the plant has sparse foliage, to keep a uniform look. If the plant has many leaves, it is okay to remove entire leaves if they are partially destroyed.

Always remove errant stems (those not showing any growth), or they will stick up and detract from the general appearance of the plant and hinder a pretty design. You can determine if a stem is dead by slightly bending it: If it is green or white inside, you know growth still exists. If it is brown or a very dried yellow in color, the stem is dead and should be removed.

Training Plants to Supports

Some plants have tendrils that will, by themselves, grasp wooden supports, string, or wire. Other plants climb by stems; the stem has a spiral growth pattern that enables it to adhere to surfaces. And some plants climb by means of the end of their leaf tips, as with, for example, the glory lily. Since nature has endowed each vine with a climbing apparatus of its own, you will rarely have to put a tendril around a pole; the plant will do this itself. What you have to do is make sure the vine is flat against the trellis, post, or string so these natural devices can work on their own.

To get plants flat against a support, tie them with nylon string or commercial tie-ons. Do this gently. Never strangle the plant. If you tie the string too tight, it will cut off circulation and end the growth of that stem.

If a vining plant becomes top- or bottom-heavy, support the heavy growth with suspender-type string designs or pieces of thin wire. This support can, if not done properly, look terrible, so learn how to do it well. Always run the string along the back of the trellis and loop it around stems to give them support. The string or wire will need anchoring at the top—I generally use a small tack or pushpin. *Never* use Scotch tape to adhere stems of plants to supports because it looks terrible and does not hold very long. (If you cut and trim stems as instructed in the beginning of this chapter, however, you should not have a top- or bottom-heavy plant.)

After a time you can probably remove all supporting devices, because the plant will have established itself in a pattern and need no more help. Gently clip away the supporting device, or you can leave it. Usually, leaves will cover the device anyway, but there is always that inquisitive guest who looks closely at everything. If comments like, "Oh, look at the string," bother you, remove the device before that particular person arrives. Because I write books about plants, people are always critical about my plants and observe them as if they were the Hope diamond, looking at every angle. I have to be meticulous; perhaps you do not.

TYING VINES

7

leafy beauties

For years ivy was considered *the* vine for indoors, with philodendron running a close second. Actually, both these vines leave a great deal to be desired as a good house plant. Ivy invariably gets red spider, even with good care, and most philodendrons (not all) eventually become straggly. So, unfortunately, vines have been considered inferior house plants; yet there are many lovely foliage vines that can make an indoor garden a cascade of colorful green.

Not all these leafy vines are true vines, but all can be trained to climb and clamber. These versatile leafy vines include cissus (kangaroo and grape ivy), scindapsus (ivy arum), pothos (a lovely green-and-yellow leaved plant), tradescantias and zebrinas (wandering Jews), and a selected group of philodendrons that will respond with care indoors and always be beautiful, with large, handsome, lush leaves. The mistletoe fig is another stellar indoor plant that can be trained to climb. And you cannot stop the tiny fig *Ficus pumila* from climbing! Another vining plant just now becoming popular is Swedish ivy (plectranthus).

But do vines need more special care than other house plants? To a degree, yes. Most vines are fast-growing plants that require a different set of rules than other, slower growing, indoor subjects. Watering, soil, feeding, temperature, and other factors *must* be considered when growing vines.

Care

The vining type plants usually grow fast; for example, if you have a plant in a 6-inch pot, within three or four months the plant will be ready for repotting. Any plant that grows this quickly needs water and food more frequently than do other plants. But first consider soil. Use a rich, porous soil, such as the house-plant soil mix available in packages. However, be careful because not all packaged mixes are superior in content, and it is hard to determine what is in them. Be sure the soil is porous and mealy to the touch; feel the package, squish it in your hand—it should feel spongy.

To this packaged soil, add some compost: 1 tablespoonful to a 6-inch pot, 2 tablespoonfuls to a 10-inch pot, and so on. Compost now comes in tidy packages, so I am not asking you to start a compost pile in a corner of the dining room. Packaged compost is expensive, but it is convenient and it makes the soil fertile and nutritious; plants need compost. (Absolutely do *not* buy soil-less mixes, which also come in packages, because they have no nutrients at all and require constant feeding.)

Once you have a good soil, plant carefully. That is, do not mishandle the plants; handle them gently. Spread out the roots, trim away dead leaves or stems, and do a neat job. Allow 1 inch of space at the top of the pot for watering, and pack down soil in and around the collar of the plant so there are no air gaps that can cause dry spots. (When roots hit dry spots, often the roots stop growing.)

Supports and frames, which we discussed in Chapter 4, are vital for vining plants. Most vining plants have tendrils or stems that look for places to grasp onto, since they naturally prefer to grow this way. The support must be kept moist, especially if you want large leaves rather than skinny ones at the tips of stems. It is not necessary to drench the trellis; merely spray it with water every day or so. This may seem a tedious process, but it is actually good for you and your plant: It makes you slow down for a few minutes and it helps keep the plant healthy.

A less-than-sunny exposure is fine for most of the plants we discuss in this chapter. Generally, vines are low light level plants that can, if necessary, survive in a northern exposure. None need direct sun, so vines are the ideal beauties for windows where nothing else will grow.

In most homes the temperature and humidity you are comfortable in will suit plants too. Basically, plants need a humidity (moisture in the air) of 30 to 50 percent; more can be harmful, and less humidity can be desiccating to the plant (and to you). Temperatures of 72° to 78°F by day with a 10 to 15 degree drop at night are fine for most plants. In fact, the variation between day and night temperature is necessary for healthy growth.

Pruning and Training

We discussed general pruning and training in the last chapter; here we are concerned with what you do when you first get a plant or when you repot it. In either case the procedure is the same. Trim away dead stems or those that do not look healthy (they may seem limp and wan). Leave only four or five strong, stout stems. If it grieves you to cut away plant parts, remember that most plants really like the pruning, because it stimulates new growth and gives them new life.

When you have trimmed the plant, tie each stem to the trellis support. When you tie, do it gently; do not strangle the stems. Use string or tie-ons. As the plant grows, securely tie new branches and shoots when they are 4 or 5 inches long. If you have the time and the ability, try to design a pattern with the leaves, so that they become individual and look whole rather than like a jungle of leaves on a wood post.

Eventually the vines will outgrow their trellises, and then what do you do? That is a good question. When vines are lush and handsome it is very difficult to cut off, say, a 12-inch piece from the very top. To avoid this, use the double-back method and train the vine downward. If you prefer not to go through this pattern making, cut the top piece off and root it in water to make a new plant. When the new plant is a few inches high, with roots, pot it at the base of the old plant to hide any bare spots that may have appeared.

Plant List

The following list of plants is by no means complete, but it does include enough foliage plants to get you vining right away. The subjects were chosen because most are easy to grow and will make you look like an experienced gardener, even if you are not. (Flowering vining plants are discussed in the next chapter.)

Aucuba goldiena

Known as the gold dust tree, this plant has striking yellow-spotted, large leaves. Although a leafy plant, it seems to adapt well to espalier growing. Trim and prune stems and leaves and tie to a trellis; use a simple pattern and do not cut too much foliage at one time; rather, do it over a long span of time. Give the plant bright light—sun is not necessary— and keep the soil evenly moist all year.

Aucuba is rather a large plant—it can grow to 60 inches—so grow it only if you have ample space. While it is not as spectacular as lantana or medinella, *A. goldiena* is still worthwhile for its leafy beauty. You will find the plant at nurseries, in the outdoor section.

Asparagus sprengeri (emerald fern)

There are several species of asparagus plants, but *A. sprengeri* has become the most popular because of its feathery fronds and pendant manner. It is a most handsome plant, and a versatile one. It can be used in hanging containers or grown against a trellis—the trellis a background for the arching stems. Tying is not usually necessary.

Grow this plant in bright light in an airy place (it dislikes a stuffy atmosphere). Allow the soil to dry out between waterings, and in case you forget to water the asparagus fern, don't panic. It has its own water storage vessels if you are neglectful. In winter it produces tiny flowers followed by red berries and is especially colorful at this time. This is a totally worthwhile plant, sure to please.

Ceropegia woodii
(string-of-hearts)

With heart-shaped leaves spaced far apart, this is a rather charming plant but will require pruning and trimming to be its best. It can become quite straggly without some help. Usually considered a shelf or basket plant, it can also be used with great effect tied to a trellis or string support to create a tapestry design.

Grow the string-of-hearts in a bright, cool place where there is a good circulation of air. The plant is somewhat temperamental about too much water, so keep the soil just evenly moist all year. While not a spectacular display, *C. woodii* has its own character and is a distinctive plant.

Cissus
(grape or kangaroo ivy)

They call these plants grape ivy or kangaroo ivy, but by any name they are handsome and are among the easiest plants for the indoor gardener to grow. They climb or trail, will grow in sun or shade, and can tolerate a dry soil if necessary—something most plants cannot tolerate. Repot cissus plants every year; they are greedy and quickly use up nutrients in soil. Not much more I can say about these; they are almost care-free.

C. antartica. Fresh, shiny green leaves with brown veining.

C. discolor. A beautiful leaved plant—green with red veins and tints of white or pink. Pretty. Slow growing.

C. rhombifolia. This is perhaps the most popular, with metallic green, brown-veined leaves.

Fatshedera lizei

This is a leafy beauty with large, green leaves and is very suitable to espalier-type growing. A shrubby plant, fatshedera is a cross between an English ivy and a fatsia. It is desirable indoors because, if necessary, it can tolerate low light levels and abuse. Foliage develops best color out of sun, with only bright light. Soak soil, but allow it to dry out between watering.

Prune and train fatshedera about once a month; do this all year. Be sure branches are tied securely flat against the trellis support. The plant adapts to pattern growing easily and, all in all, makes a fine display where a green accent is needed. It is ideal for a large divider or screen area.

Fatshedera is another outdoor plant, so you will find it at nurseries. The species name is *F. lizei*. There is also a variegated form, with yellow-and-green leaves, but it is somewhat more difficult to grow than the standard green type.

Ficus

This group of plants includes the popular banyan indoor tree and the often overlooked creeping fig (*Ficus pumila*). The creeping fig, with tiny, green, paper-thin leaves, almost grows by itself once it finds a spot to its liking. Put it in bright but not sunny areas. Keep soil somewhat moist. *F. pumila* needs support and will clamber on glass, wood,

Cissus rhombifolia

Fatshedera lizei

Ficus pumila

stone—anything. It is a good plant for the beginner because it rarely fails. Trim away leaves to establish the pattern desired.

F. diversifolia (mistletoe fig). Round leaves and a lovely branching habit. Very pretty.

F. radicans variegata. Pointed, variegated leaves; a climber.

Hedera helix (ivy)

People either adore ivy or hate it, and there seems to be no in-between. Unfortunately, I fall in the second category, for no matter what kind of ivy or how I grow it, red spider soon demolishes the plant. But my failures could be your successes, and because ivy makes such a lovely display it must be considered as a desirable plant. I have grown ivy in sun, in shade, with lots of water, with little water, and while the plant grows luxuriantly it rarely lasts over a year for me. For you, I hope it lives a long time. There are numerous varieties, one prettier than the other. The popular species is *H. hedera*.

Jasminum (jasmine)

We know these are scented plants for outdoors, but they are equally valuable indoors. Most have white, small flowers and pretty, dark-green leaves. Jasmines are twiners and climbers and grow rather quickly; they are nice if you want a green effect in a few months.

Give plants a bright place and some sun in winter. Keep soil quite moist at all times, and occasionally spray plants with tepid water. Jasmines can climb to enormous heights, so be prepared: have suitable trellises in place. The plants are not fussy about temperature or humidity.

J. mesyni. A jasmine that is more shrubby than climbing, with yellow flowers and light-green, lance-shaped leaves. Scented.

J. nudiflorum. This is a nonclimbing jasmine—more a shrub—from China. The flowers are yellow, with handsome leaves. I mention this one so you will not get it confused with the vining ones. Still nice to grow indoors.

J. officinale. A climber from Persia. It has small, white flowers that bloom from July to the dark fall months, making this plant quite desirable. Its handsome green leaves tend to die back occasionally; if they do, just reduce water and let the plant recover by itself.

J. sambac. This jasmine has broad, oval leaves and small, white flowers. It does not seem to be as robust as the other jasmines mentioned here. Some improved varieties are available. Very fragrant.

Jasminum

49

Philodendron cordatum

Manettia inflata
(Mexican firecracker)

This is a climbing plant that grows to 24 inches, with small, tubular, red-tipped flowers. It requires sun. Allow soil to dry out between waterings. Manettia thrives when potbound and needs a location where there is a good circulation of air. Only one species is available, *M. inflata*.

Philodendron

This is a large group of plants, with many vining species, some good, some not so good. However, most philodendrons have the advantage of being able to tolerate low light levels; this makes the plants ideal for most

homes. Keep soil evenly moist; feed biweekly (except in winter) and provide a stake, pole, or trellis for plants to vine on. Without suitable supports, philodendrons simply become straggly and unattractive. They must be kept trimmed and trained to pleasing patterns.

P. andreanum. Velvety, dark-green leaves with copper tinge and white veins.

P. 'Burgundy.' A hybrid with wine-red, lance-shaped leaves. A robust grower.

P. cordatum. Perhaps the most popular philodendron, with heart-shaped leaves. A fast grower.

50

Philodendron laciniatum

P. hastatum. Popular, with
medium-sized, arrow-shaped leaves.

P. panduraeforme. Splendid
fiddleleaf, leathery, olive-green
leaves.

P. laciniatum. A handsome
lobed-leaved beauty.

P. variifolium. Heart-shaped leaves,
olive-green. Somewhat small.

P. verrucosum. Large, arrow-shaped,
dark-green, almost crinkled, leaves.
A beauty.

P. radiatum. A good viner with
dark-green, large-lobed leaves.

Philodendron variifolium

Philodendron verrucosum

52

Plectranthus

Plectranthus (Swedish ivy)

With heart-shaped, toothed leaves, these trailers or climbers do very well in the home, especially if the light is not the very best. The plants grow fast and, as a result, can become somewhat straggly, so trim and prune them to keep them bushy and symmetrical. While growth is vinelike, these are not true vines and require some time to train to a trellis or other support. Yet they look best grown in this way rather than having a mass of tangled leaves. Keep plectranthus evenly moist all year.

P. australis. Typical plectranthus, with waxy, toothed leaves. Grows quickly.

P. oertendahli. Somewhat more distinct than most species, with handsome apple-green leaves, veined silver. My choice.

Saxifraga
(strawberry begonia)

With geraniumlike leaves and strawberry coloring, these are trailing plants with very handsome, heart-shaped scalloped leaves. Plants produce long runners, making them good trailing/vine plants. Give saxifragas even moisture all year, except in winter, when they can be grown somewhat dry.

S. sarmentosa. Small reddish leaves, veined white.

S. s. 'Tricolor.' Dark-green, rosy-red, and white leaves.

Scindapsus (pothos)

This is a climber or viner, with smooth, dark-green leaves splashed yellow or white. Pothos grows like a weed in almost any situation. It is highly recommended for the beginner because it needs almost no care.

S. aureus. Dark-green leaves, laced yellow.

S. a. 'Marble Queen.' Green leaves, streaked white.

S. a. 'Silver Moon.' Creamy yellow foliage.

S. pictus argyraeus. Satiny green leaves, edged silver.

Syngonium podophyllum
(arrowhead plant)

This is a plant that appears now and then at suppliers (and is often called nephthytis). It has arrow-shaped, green leaves, sometimes variegated, and is a trailing plant by nature. The plant grows quickly and is easily trained to a support; indeed, it grows too fast and can become a mass of leaves, which is hardly attractive. So have pruning shears on hand to keep it in bounds.

Undaunted by adversity, syngonium seems to flourish in any condition, but ideally it likes a bright place and a somewhat wet soil. Cut back the plant every so often to about 6 inches to encourage a new crop of leaves. Even a rank beginner will be a successful gardener with the arrowhead plant. There have been some very pretty variegated forms recently introduced, such as *S. podophyllum* 'Emerald Gem' and *S. podophyllum* 'Imperial White.'

Tolmiea (piggyback plant)

This is a creeping, clambering plant that bears new plants on the back of old leaves, thus earning its common name. Leaves are light green. This plant needs buckets of water to grow well. Piggybacks can be trained upright, but this is very difficult, so grow them as trailers for dividers or screens. One species is generally offered: *T. menziesii.*

Syngonium

Tradescantia (wandering Jew)

These plants are perhaps the most popular trailing plants grown today. They can also be trained to grow upward. There has been such a proliferation of tradescantias lately that it is hard to keep up with new ones. Some are solid green, others are green-and-white, some are almost red, still others are wine red and black-green leaved, and there is a most charming tiny-leaved tradescantia, succulent in texture. The beauty of tradescantias is that they grow and grow and grow. Keep soil moist and give plants a bright place—that is about all there is to it.

T. blossfeldiana. Green foliage with silver hairs.

T. fuminensis. Green leaves, and probably the most commonly grown wandering Jew. *T. f. albo-vittata* has blue-green and white leaves.

T. laekenensis. A very colorful plant, with green-and-pink leaves.

T. navicularis. A beauty with small, green, almost boat-shaped leaves.

Zebrina

The plants in this group resemble tradescantias. Native to Mexico, these gems are trailing plants that grow quickly and become a mass of color in a short time. Keep soil evenly moist and grow plants in sun or shade. Zebrinas train easily against a trellis or on a wall.

Z. pendula. Lovely purple leaves with silver bands; arching stems.

Z. p. 'Discolor.' Brown leaves with purple-and-white stripes.

Z. p. 'Quadricolor.' Purple-green leaves banded white and striped pink and purple. Very colorful; highly recommended.

Sweet Potato

The common old sweet potato makes a very handsome indoor plant, even if it lasts only a few months. To start a sweet potato, place the bottom half in water—use a mayonnaise jar that is large enough to allow the potato to rest on the rim. In a short time, roots form and leaves sprout and keep sprouting and the vine becomes longer and longer—it is beautiful. Most sweet potato growers let the plant grow naturally pendant, but some indoor gardeners use trellises for the potato; they tie the stems to the supports. When you select potatoes, be sure they are already sprouting, that is, have little nodules on them. Some potatoes are sprayed with a growth inhibitor that makes them difficult, if not impossible, to grow.

8

flowering gems

Twenty years ago, after growing many foliage plants at home, I decided there was little reason flowering plants would not do as well. At the time, the idea of growing orchids or bougainvilleas indoors was considered ridiculous. I relegated my foliage plants to other areas of the home and started growing thunbergias, allamanda, and a few other outdoor flowering plants I felt would adapt to indoors. There just was not anything else available.

In a few years I had accumulated a collection of beautiful plants that bore colorful blossoms throughout the year. In fact, I wrote one of my first books, *Flowering House Plants, Month by Month,* to prove it could be done. Today, many flowering plants are part of indoor greeneries, and the vining and climbing types include many that can add fine color to your home. Actually, there seems to be more flowering varieties than foliage plants among the vining and trailing plants.

Twenty years ago, I had difficulty finding my plants, but today you will have little problem locating them.

Most of these plants are available from house-plant suppliers or, for the more specialized plants like schizocentron, from mail-order suppliers throughout the country.

Care

Make no mistake about it: flowering plants need more care than do foliage ones. They need ample sun, misting, more feeding, and more grooming, and when in bud, protection from fluctuating temperatures. Despite all these time-consuming tasks, flowering plants are worth their weight in gold indoors. There is nothing that can add as much cheer or color to a home as bright lantanas or brilliant clerodendrum blossoms. There is truly a wealth of beauty here that you should not miss.

Use packaged house-plant soil mix and add some compost or humus to it, as described under "Care" in Chapter 7. One more thing: add 1 tablespoonful of bone meal to plants in pots up to 6 inches in diameter and 2 tablespoonfuls to plants in larger pots. Be sure all containers have drainage holes, and when you repot plants (flowering plants need more frequent repotting than do foliage ones), pack down the soil so that there are no air pockets.

Choose a bright, sunny window for flowering plants—an east, south, or west window (in that order of preference). If all you have is a north light, stick to the foliage plants. Good humidity of at least 40 percent is necessary for blooming plants. Although average daytime home temperatures are fine, most flowering species need cooler night temperatures, about 55° to 60°F. Keep a good ventilation of air going through the growing area at all times, because a stagnant situation will kill plants quickly. Mist plants with tepid water often.

Like foliage plants, vining, flowering ones adapt well to trellis or wood-stake growing, or they can also be grown on string or wire. Train plants as we already described, or just place plants at the corners of shelves and bookcase units wherever color is needed.

It is important that you pick off flowers as soon as they fade, because dead flowers are an invitation to fungus diseases, which can wipe out a collection.

Types and Kinds of Plants

Some vining, flowering subjects will adapt to wall growing better than others—stephanotis is a prime example of a good vining plant.

Rusellias are more trailing in habit and thus should be used for the screen and divider areas. Allamanda is a very large climber and needs ample space to ramble, so try it only if you can give it room. Bougainvillea, with its vivid red bracts, is fine but really needs weekly pruning and training to make it look its best.

Trailing lantanas and geraniums can be used as trailers, or grow them up a trellis. Clerodendrum with bright red and white flowers, needs string support.

There are so many flowering plants of varying habit that it is wise to start growing a few and decide just what will do right in your home. There are small plants and large ones, climbers and trailers and true vines. And do not forget to grow some nasturtiums and morning glories, for indoor sights you will never forget. These are really outdoor flowers, but believe me, they perform indoors too, perhaps with less flowers but enough blooms to make any area a dramatic place.

Aeschynanthus (lipstick vine)

These are popular trailing plants with lovely red, brown, or orange flowers. The plants have closely set leaves and can grow to 48 inches. Keep these vines out of the sun; it will burn them. Instead, put them in a bright place and give them even moisture all year. Lipstick vines take a while to acclimatize to new conditions, and it may be several months before a plant regains its vigor and starts to perform. In any case, use them for hanging baskets, or you can also train them on a trellis or string support by tying stems to the wood or string.

A. lobbianus. Fine red flowers, dark-green leaves.

A. marmoratus. Greenish-brown flowers; grows more easily than others mentioned here.

A. speciosus. Most popular, with orange-red flowers.

Allamanda

Evergreen climbers, allamandas are vines with large, green leaves and waxy flowers in spring and summer. Give the plants full sun and plenty of water when they are growing. In winter, keep the soil barely moist. You will have to trim the plants back severely in spring to keep them in bounds. These are not easy plants to grow indoors but are worth the space if you have a large sunny area where accent is needed. Provide a substantial support for the plants and keep them trained and tied properly.

A. nerifolia. Large and beautiful, with bright-yellow flowers.

A. violacea. Dramatic plant, with reddish-purple flowers.

Antigonon (queen's wreath)

These prolific flowering climbers like heat and sun. The flowers, which look like pink begonias, are produced in long trailing sprays; they bloom on and off throughout the warm months. Keep the plants well watered all year, except in winter, when they need a slightly dry rest. Plants need frequent pruning and training and really grow rapidly, so do not feed them. The species usually available is *Antigonon leptopus.*

Begonia

This is such a large family of plants that it is difficult to single out special plants. Begonias are usually classified as fibrous, hirsute, rhizomatous, and angel-wing. The angel-wings, with pendant growth and clusters of bright flowers, are perhaps the best for your purposes, although years ago I had a fine rhizomatous begonia that literally covered a wall. Most begonias like some sun but not too much heat and seem to revel in moisture, so keep soil quite moist. Popular angel-wings include *B.* 'Gray Feather,' with white flowers; *B.* 'Orange Rubra,' with orange blossoms; and *B.* 'Elvira Swisher,' with pink flowers.

Bougainvillea

For years I grew this lovely vine in the plant room, where it got ample sun and heat—the plant was gorgeous. This vision of beauty ended because the plant became so large and heavy that one day it slipped from its mooring and crashed to the floor; it has never been the same since. The trick with bougainvillea, if there is one, is to get it established; then it takes off on its

Bougainvillea

own. Give the plant plenty of water and mist it frequently. Bougainvillea is a greedy but beautiful plant. *B*. 'Barbara Karst' and 'San Diego Red' are the best choices.

Brunfelsia calycina floribunda (yesterday-today-and-tomorrow)

Rangy in growth and difficult to grow *B. calycina floribunda* is still worth your time. It is a winter-blooming plant that bears pretty purple, fragrant flowers that turn white about a week after opening. Foliage is green and bushy, and the sprawling growth habit makes the plant ideal for espaliering.

Grow brunfelsia in bright light and keep the soil evenly moist all year.

Keep pinching shoots back to encourage fresh growth, and feed every other watering with a weak fertilizer. The plant earned its common name because the flowers go through three stages of coloring, and thus poetically we have a yesterday-today-and-tomorrow plant.

Clerodendrum (glory bower)

These bushy, vining plants have handsome large, dark-green leaves and splendid red-and-white flowers, a veritable treasure of color. Mature plants are a stunning sight, and even if you start with a small clerodendrum (in a 6-inch pot), within one year it will be 30 to 40 inches tall.

60

Train the vines to wood supports or string. Plants will make a dense covering, and flowers may appear in spring or in summer. Allow soil to dry out between waterings; coolness at night will help promote good growth. An outstanding plant well worth your time, it is technically called *C. thomsonae*.

Cobea scandens (cup-and-saucer vine)

This is an often overlooked vine that is very attractive, with bright-green, oval leaves and pretty violet flowers that are bell-shaped. The plant blooms from midsummer until fall. It is a rapid grower and clings to any rough surface or trellis by its tendrils, rather than by the vine twining.

Grow plants in ample sun; give them large pots of rich soil kept evenly moist. Cobea can take a lot of water. Plants are difficult to buy, and in most cases you will have to start your own from seed yearly. Seeds are available.

Columnea

These gesneriads offer a fine selection of flowering plants, including trailers, climbers, and upright growers. The foliage varies in size and color, but is always handsome, and the flowers in bright colors are exciting.

The plants like a somewhat sunny place (with protection from noonday

61

sun). Keep soil evenly moist, and when plants are growing well in spring and summer, feed every other watering with a 10–10–5 plant food. Some columneas can grow to large size with sprawling branches; these are the ones for wall and trellis growing; tie stems to supports and keep plants trimmed and pruned.

C. arguta. Bright orange flowers.

C. microphylla. A beautiful, yellow-flowering species, with small leaves.

Other varieties include *C.* 'Yellow Dragon' and *C.* 'Butterball,' both beautiful.

Dipladenia (Mexican love vine)

These charming vines adapt well to trellis growing and offer bright funnel-shaped, pink flowers throughout the summer months. The plants require a warm, sunny place to do their best and take buckets of water. Keep soil moist all the time, except in winter when it can be somewhat dry, but never bone dry. These are twining plants that will grow to any wood support, and grow fast—a small plant can become a large one in one season. The species name is *D. amoena.*

Euphorbia milii (crown-of-thorns)

You need a stout heart and heavy leather gloves to train *E. milii* (commonly known as the crown-of-thorns) in an espalier pattern. But it is a plant that has a rather sparse growth habit and not much pruning or training is really required. Indeed, with some judicious pruning, you may not have to tie the plant in place but rather just place it in front of the trellis.

From the euphorbia family—the same family that gives us the Christmas poinsettia—*E. milii* bears little resemblance to its cousin. It is a branching plant with thick stems covered with thorns, and small, dark-green leaves and vivid red bracts. Mature specimens can become decorative accents in the home because they are so handsome.

Grow the plant in a sandy soil and allow the soil to dry out between waterings. Overwatering can kill it, so always keep soil on the dry side. Give sunlight in winter; at other times, bright light is all that is needed. If you do have to prune a few branches, be sure to seal the cuts with charcoal to avoid any possibility of disease entering the cells.

Geranium

The ivy-leaved geraniums with vivid flowers are excellent indoor plants. As I am writing this, one is blooming in the small greenhouse—it has been blooming for months. Looking at my geranium, I realize it has grown so fast that it already needs training and tying. (I'll give it a support of wood sticks or a string trellis to keep it handsome.) The plant likes plenty of water and good sunlight. Just ask for ivy-leaved geraniums at suppliers.

Euphorbia milii

Gloriosa (glory lily)

These are bulbous plants with large, exotic red-and-orange flowers in summer. Start the bulb in a rich soil; plant it about 1 inch below the soil, and keep it just moist until leaves are up about 10 inches. Then increase moisture, and give the plant full sun. The glory lily climbs by a unique method: The ends of the leaves have grasping tendrils. Thus the plant needs string or wire support. When the bloom is over, store the pot in a dry, cool (60°F) place for replanting the following year; when you repot, use fresh soil. Ask for the glory lily by its botanical name, *G. rothschildiana*.

Hibiscus

This venerable outdoor favorite can be a good indoor plant too—especially welcome because it blooms on and off through fall and winter with large, handsome flowers. Hibiscus can be trained to a support and does very well when grown in this manner. Tie branches to a vertical screen and watch it grow. It is especially good for espalier growing.

The plant requires a great deal of water. It definitely needs sun; without it, the harvest of flowers will be sparse, if you get any at all. Feed every other watering with a 10–10–5 plant food, and watch leaves for spider mites, which have a fondness for the plant. There are a number of varieties available, one prettier than the other, but my favorite color is orange. Look for hibiscus at nurseries, in the outdoor section.

Hoya (wax plant)

These old favorites have been popular for years, and rightly so, because a mature, well-grown wax plant is a sight indeed. The oval leaves are dark green and handsome; the flower clusters are waxy, beautiful, and fragrant. The problem is that hoyas will not bloom until they are mature.

Grow the wax plant in a somewhat sandy soil and let it dry out between waterings. Do not remove stems or spurs on which flowers have been produced, because they are sources of next season's bloom. Plants need good sun and average temperatures. These plants have been hybridized extensively, so insist on the *original* wax plant, *H. carnosa.*

Ipomoea (morning glory)

These outdoor plants do very well indoors, and the wealth of flowers, one following the other throughout the summer months, is quite cheerful. Morning glories need very large containers and tons of water. Give plants a support or they will become a horrible tangle, because the plants vine around almost any object. Generally, you cannot buy these plants started, so you will have to start from seed (as outlined in

Chapter 10). Morning glories are only good for one season but are well worth the space because of their magnificent color. They come in a beautiful blue ('Heavenly Blue') or white ('Pearly White'), and there is also a cerise-flowering type.

Lantana

There are many lantanas, but the one we want to grow in espalier fashion is known as *L. montevidensis,* and a finer plant is hard to find. Often overlooked, lantana offers small, green leaves and clusters of delightful lavender flowers on and off throughout the year indoors, especially in fall and winter.

The plant is rangy and needs training. Give it buckets of water in summer and fall, not so much moisture the rest of the year. Temperatures of 60°F suit this trailing beauty, and sun will assure a good crop of flowers.

If you want a distinctive plant, one that isn't seen often but offers a great deal, this is the plant for you.

Medinella (love plant)

This is a lush green plant with large, green leaves and panicles of carmine flowers in pink brackets. Blossoming can occur any time of the year, but only with mature plants. Grow in bright light. Water moderately except in winter, then only twice a week. Train and tie to a trellis as required, and prune errant branches in the early spring.

This is a difficult plant to find, and

often you will have to buy small specimens from a mail-order supplier and grow them into mature plants. Still, because of its beauty, it is worth the time. *Medinella magnifica* is the species you want.

Passiflora (passion flower)

Passion flowers are well known because of their large, complex, and colorful flowers, but they are by no means easy plants to bring to perfection indoors. Passifloras need pampering. Be sure plants are in large tubs—they refuse to grow in small pots—and give plants a somewhat cool location. The plants like some

but not too much sun, and although passion flowers need lots of water, too much can harm them. Treat these plants gently and nicely, and you will have flowers.

The problem with these vining plants is that once they do get going, they grow so quickly that they can cover a wall. Keep passifloras in bounds by frequent pruning. If you have a large area or a greenhouse, by all means try these unusual vines; if you live in an apartment, stick with dependable beauties like dipladenias.

Good passion flowers include *P. alato-caerulea* (most popular), *P. jamesonii* (rose or coral-red flowers), and *P. edulis* (purpie flowers).

Passiflora

Plumbago capensis
(leadwort)

With the terrible common name of leadwort, this is a beautiful, 30-inch shrub of rangy growth that bears clusters of delightful blue flowers on and off throughout the year. A mature specimen in bloom is a breathtaking sight, and the sprawling growth pattern can easily be kept in bounds, trained to a trellis. It is especially good for espalier growing.

In active growth—during the summer—plumbago needs buckets of water and full sun. Feed with a 10–10–5 fertilizer every other watering. In autumn the plant will naturally slow down in growth; this is the time to taper off water, but never allow the soil to be bone dry. During winter, keep plumbago barely moist.

Sometime in February, cut and prune to pattern drastically. This will encourage a new flush of growth. Mist the foliage in warm weather to keep leaves clean and healthy (and to help avoid an attack of red spider, which have a fondness for this plant).

You will find plumbago in the outdoor section of nurseries—it is basically an outdoor shrub and is generally inexpensive. The species you want is *P. capensis*.

Ruellia

These are very desirable plants because they bear their red flowers in fall and winter, when color is needed at a window. The plants have dark-green leaves and need ample sun to bear a harvest of flowers. Keep the soil just barely moist; these plants are sensitive to overwatering. These are not natural viners and will need some help; train them to a support.

R. amoena. Waxy, oval leaves and fine, bright-red flowers.

R. macrantha. Dark-green leaves and lovely, rose-colored blooms.

Schizocentron (Spanish shawl)

You have probably never heard of this creeping plant, but you will bless me for telling you about it. It is a mass of little green leaves and cherry-purple flowers, absolutely exquisite when grown properly. The plant is not a viner or a trailer but a creeper. It needs only watering and a sunny place to thrive. *S. elegans* is the species you want.

Stephanotis (Madagascar jasmine)

This dark-green leaved beauty is not easy to coax to bloom, but the waxy white, heavily scented flowers are worth every effort. Madagascar jasmine can grow to 15 feet and thus will need a sturdy support. Mist frequently and keep the soil evenly moist. To bloom, stephanotis needs coolness (55° to 60°F) at night. The only available species is *S. floribunda*.

Stephanotis floribunda

67

Thunbergia
(black-eyed Susan)

Undoubtedly you have seen this handsome plant growing outdoors. Indoors, in a sunny, warm place, it will be just as free with its brilliant orange, black-centered flowers. Thunbergia is really a fast-growing, twining plant that can take over in a short time; it attaches to anything at hand.

T. alata. Yellow or orange 3-inch flowers with a dark center.

T. erecta. More erect than *T. alata.*

T. grandiflora. A find if you can search out one. Large, blue flowers in the fall.

Tropaeolum (nasturtium)

These lovely orange beauties grow almost wild outdoors in my garden and reseed themselves year after year. I started my nasturtiums indoors several years ago; now I grow a few pots because of the fantastic color. I start seeds every year in a 12-inch pot of poor soil and let them go. Plants germinate quickly, and flowers appear on and off throughout the year. Nasturtiums need plenty of water and sun to do their best. You can use the regular garden varieties, or buy species like *T. speciosum* or *T. pentaphyllum;* the latter plants need more care and patience to get them growing but are beautiful and worth the trouble.

Vanilla

Do you like orchids? Vanilla is an exquisitely handsome one. It has thick oval leaves, and it will vine around any type of support. Vanilla needs high humidity and no sunlight; it prefers a shady, moist place. Plant vanilla in equal parts of soil and crushed firbark. This is one of the slowest vines I have ever grown, barely making 6 inches of growth each year, but if you have the patience—and it takes about 7 years—you will be rewarded beyond your wildest dreams. Vanilla bears huge (7-inch), brilliant yellow flowers in the heat of summer. Vanilla is something to see, and once it is established, it will bloom yearly. A truly beautiful but somewhat tempermental plant, for the person with patience. The botanical name is *V. planifolia.*

PROTECTING THE GREEN

If you grow house plants, you will want to protect them from insect attacks or diseases. In many of my books I have said that a healthy plant is a happy one, and this is quite true. Insects and disease rarely attack robust, healthy plants—they are just too strong. Insects go for the weaklings. And even if a strong plant has a few insects, it is easy to get rid of them, because the plant has enough stamina to resist infection and a few eaten leaves. But weak ones cannot survive an onslaught of insects.

The first line of precaution against bugs is to take care of your plants to the best of your ability so they are strong and healthy. But none of us is perfect, and occasionally we forget to water or feed a plant. Insects may hit the plant, so it is wise to know what to do and what insects to expect. Only if you know the culprit can you find the proper preventative for it.

Observation

If you like plants, you are going to look at them frequently. I do this every morning, not only because I enjoy the overall visual effect of many plants in a room, but also because I like to look at each plant as an individual entity. So through the years I have developed a sort of 1-2-3 program as I walk through the greenery. I look at (1) leaves, (2) stems, and (3) general appearance of the plant.

The leaf axils are where most insects are liable to gather, because it is an easy place for them to hide. The leaves themselves, especially underneath, are where insects will also migrate, so I inspect these as I take my morning indoor stroll. (By the way, outdoors, natural predators will take care of many insects; indoors, you or Mother Nature are the predator.) Then I look at the general appearance of the plant, as a doctor looks at the general overall appearance of patients when they come for a checkup.

As I observe the plant, if I do see signs of insects at work, I make note of which insects they are. Symptoms of insects at work can be anything from yellow or silvery leaves, to dried leaves, to limp growth, and so on. In practically all cases, the insects that will be a problem are, in order of their hazard: aphids, mealybugs, red spiders, thrips, and scale. There are, of course, other insects, but these are the main ones that attack indoor plants.

These insects can be eliminated easily if you catch them early. Only when insects have established a beachhead is there a problem of getting rid of them. It is imperative that you eliminate insects quickly; most breed very fast, and if neglected a few days, they can cause considerable trouble.

Ants are one group of insects not technically harmful to plants, but ants are insect herders. That is, they corral colonies of aphids and scale on plants for the purpose of collecting the sugars that are exuded when the insects start their work. Ants may be the first culprits to give you a hint that plants are being attacked by mealybugs, aphids, or other critters. Watch out for ants—they are not as harmless as you may think.

Prevention

There are numerous ways to eliminate insects if you see them at work. You can use chemicals, but I advise against this procedure in the home because the chemical smell is obnoxious and poisons in the home are hazardous. (However, I will talk about chemicals for plant prevention, because some people do use them.) Other ways of getting rid of insects are more in keeping with natural gardening. I use natural preventatives like laundry soap and water to eliminate aphids. Old tobacco steeped in water will eliminate scale. Alcohol on cotton swabs gets rid of mealybugs, and boiling water on soil will kill thrips and whiteflies. And a simple blast of water applied frequently will chase away any insects.

One more important natural method: I wipe leaves with a damp (water) cloth whenever I can. This eliminates more insects and eggs than you think.

If I am forced to use a preventative in the home (the infestation may be too much to handle with natural methods), I use natural chemicals like Rotenone and Pyrethrum, which are derived from plants themselves and are not as poisonous as manmade chemicals.

I try to avoid manmade chemicals like Malathion. However, if you use them for convenience and speed—and they will eliminate insects quicker than other methods—keep them out of the reach of children and pets. Avoid house-plant-insect aerosol cans; these really do a poor job of eliminating insects and are expensive.

After you use any preventative, natural or chemical, be sure to rinse plants thoroughly with tepid water. And before you use preventatives, make sure the plant has a moist soil.

Insects to Know (or Not to Know)

The following is a list of the most common insects that are liable to attack plants and what to do about them:

APHIDS: Typical aphids are pear-shaped, small soft-bodied insects, with beaks that have needlelike stylets. The aphids use these daggers to pierce plant tissue and suck out plant juices. Aphids may be black, red, green, or gray in color.
Treatment: Rotenone

MEALYBUGS: These are the cottony accumulations we see in leaf axils or on leaf veins. Mealybugs have soft, segmented bodies dressed in cottony wax. They have beaks that they insert in plants to get sap; as the sap leaves your plant, it wilts.
Treatment: Malathion or Pyrethrum

RED SPIDER MITES: These are tiny, oval creatures, hardly visible, and may be yellow, green, red, or brown. They have long legs and spin webs. If foliage turns pale and strippled, mites are probably at work.
Treatment: Diazinon or Isotox

SCALE: Scale are tiny, oval, armored shells and may be brown or black. They attach to a plant part and usually stay in one place. Plants with scale show leaf as well as stem damage.
Treatment: Malathion or Isotox

THRIPS: Thrips are chewing, small, slender insects with two pairs of narrow wings. They are usually dark in color, and their mouths are fitted with "tools" to pierce or rasp leaves.

Thrips are indicated by a silver sheen on foliage.
Treatment: Malathion or Isotox

Preventatives

The treatments mentioned above, in the insect section, are poisonous chemicals, and their mention does not indicate I suggest their use. On the contrary, I try to avoid using any chemical insecticides in the home. However, to be complete, the book must have these remedies, and whether you use them or not is up to you. In any case, with chemical preventatives you will either have to spray the preparation or, if you use the granular type, apply it to soil and then water the soil.

No matter what poison you use (if any), do follow the directions on the package to the letter, and keep poisons out of the reach of children and pets. You should also follow these basic rules:

1. Never use a chemical on a plant that is bone dry.
2. Never spray plants in direct sunlight.
3. Use sprays at the proper distance, noted on the package.
4. Try to douse insects if they are in sight.
5. Don't use chemicals in a closed room; find a well-ventilated place.

Old-Fashioned Remedies

If you prefer not to use chemicals in the home, you can use, as I do, the old-fashioned methods of eliminating insects from plants. They are perhaps not as thorough as chemicals, but they are safe and avoid noxious odors in the home (and they are also inexpensive.

HANDPICKING: This is hardly pleasant, but it can be done with a toothpick or a used toothbrush.

SOAP–AND–WATER: For many insects, such as aphids and mealybugs, a solution of ½ pound of laundry soap (*not* detergent) and water works fine. Douse or spray the mixture on the bugs, and repeat twice a week for three weeks.

ALCOHOL: Use regular rubbing alcohol on cotton swabs; apply directly to the insect. This will kill mealybugs and aphids. Repeat several times.

TOBACCO: Use a solution of old tobacco from cigarettes steeped for several days in water. It will get rid of scale and mealybugs. Repeat several times, and always rinse the plant with tepid water after application.

WATER SPRAY: This may sound ineffective, but it works quite well to rid plants of insect eggs you can't see. Use it frequently on plants, with strong enough force to wash away insects.

WIPING LEAVES FREQUENTLY: This simple step goes a long way to reduce the insect population. Use a damp cloth and wipe leaves.

Plant Diseases

"Plant disease" always sounds formidable; actually, if plants are well cared for, diseases rarely develop. However, just in case, it is wise to have a brief resume of plant diseases.

Ailments that strike plants are manifested in visible symptoms such as spots, rots, and mildew. The diseases are caused by bacteria and fungi that enter the plant through natural minute openings or through wounds. Once inside, they multiply and break down tissue. Fungus diseases also include rusts, mildew, some leaf spots, and blights. Space does not allow me to go into or thoroughly explain these diseases, but there are remedies, called fungicides. These chemicals kill or inhibit the growth of bacteria and fungi. They come in dust form (ready to use) or in wettable powders. The following are some of the fungicides available for plants. (Always use these with caution, and follow the directions on the package.)

BENOMYL: A systemic used for many bacterial and fungal maladies.

CAPTAN: An organic fungicide that is generally safe and effective for the control of many plant diseases.

KARATHANE: Highly effective for powdery mildew.

ZINEB: Used for many bacterial and fungus diseases.

STARTiNG YOUR OWN plANTS

Only recently have people begun to realize how valuable, yet inexpensive, it is to start their own plants from seed or cuttings or from division rather than buying new plants. And starting your own plants has another advantage: It gives you a certain satisfaction to raise a very tiny plant to a mature one. Like children, your own plants will always be the best.

Plant propagation is really quite simple; it is only the technical jargon that has disturbed and prevented people from trying it. But propagation can be as simple as taking a cutting of a plant, putting it in water, and then planting it once it is rooted.

Seed starting, too, requires little work—simply put some seeds in a starting medium. Because some of the vining plants we talk about cannot be purchased from suppliers (for example, dipladenias or clerodendrums), it is important for you, the vining gardener, to become involved in starting your own plants.

Sowing Seed

Starting your own plants from seed requires more patience than skill.

There are really only a few things that must be done to get the process going. You will need shallow pots or planters and a sterile starting medium like perlite or vermiculite. These mediums are packaged at suppliers, and for starting seeds they have proved far better than soil, which can contain disease organisms. You will also have to have a fairly warm, bright spot for seeds; most seeds germinate in *constant* day and night temperatures of 78°F. And, of course, seeds need moisture.

Fill the container with 3 or 4 inches of starting medium, and imbed seeds in the medium. Place large seeds directly below the surface of the perlite or vermiculite; scatter smaller seeds on top of the medium and then cover seeds with a sprinkling of the medium.

Keep the seed bed moist. Gently mist the seed bed with water; never keep it too dry or too moist. Dryness—even for a day—in the seed bed can kill small seeds. You might also want to cover the seed bed with a plastic bag propped on four sticks, to provide humidity. If you do this, be sure the medium does not retain too much moisture, which may cause damping-off, a fungus disease that kills seeds. If you see condensation on the inside of the plastic, remove the bag for a few hours.

Some seeds, such as morning glory, germinate in a few days, but other seeds take weeks. You will know the seed has germinated when the first true leaves show. Leave the seedlings in the container, but when they reach 2 or 3 inches, thin out some seedlings so the others have space to grow. When the seedlings are 3 to 5 inches high, transplant them.

To transplant seedlings, pick them out with a blunt-edged stick or pencil; be gentle (do not break the roots). Put the seedlings in separate containers to grow. Some gardeners replant again in community seed beds (many plants to a container) and wait until plants are 8 to 10 inches tall before individual planting, but this is generally not necessary.

Not all the seeds you sow will germinate, but the odds are in your favor. Quite frankly, you will not want dozens of plantlets anyway, and since seed is inexpensive, sowing seed is really a fine way to get new plants inexpensively. There is another plus about starting your own seed: The plants you start are accustomed to your indoor conditions and thus do not have to go through a transition shock. Plants you buy grown in greenhouses under ideal conditions must adapt to the shock and recover.

Plants From Cuttings

At a north window I always keep a mayonnaise jar filled with water and a few charcoal chips. (Charcoal helps keep the water sweet.) When vines get too long, I merely snip off the top 6 inches, remove the bottom two leaves, and put the cutting in the water. Some cuttings form roots in a few weeks; others do not. But even if my average is three out of five, I am way ahead of the game.

For better results, put the cutting in a starting medium. Take cuttings in the spring or early summer, which is the plant's natural growth time. In fall and winter the cutting is less likely to strike roots. Any household container like a frozen roll carton, cottage cheese carton, or milk carton cut lengthwise and filled with starting medium can be used for cuttings. Use 3 or 4 inches of vermiculite in the container; dip the end of the cutting in a rooting hormone (to help it sprout), and put it in the growing medium. Put a plastic bag over the cutting to ensure good humidity and keep the medium moist. Put the cutting in a warm place (75°F). In a few weeks, remove the plastic bag, pull out a cutting, and see if roots have formed. If they have, transplant the cutting to a 3-inch pot of soil to grow. (If the cutting does not have roots, replace it and wait.)

Plant Offshoots and Division

Some plants, like chlorophytums, produce *offshoots* (stolons) at their bases. Offshoots are small plants, replicas of the mother plant. When the babies are about 4 inches long and show fresh green growth, remove them from the parent plant and start them in separate containers of vermiculite or a mixture of sand and soil. To remove an offshoot, use a sterile knife and make a clean, slanting cut. Keep the offshoots in a warm (75°F), bright place. In about a month, start a feeding program with 10–10–5 plant food every other watering. Some plants grow quickly and others take months to reach potting stage, so be patient.

Division means to divide a large plant to make two plants. You can do this only with plants that have crowns. Simply pull apart or cut in half the large plant to make two plants. For example, when you look down at a clerodendrum from the top, you can almost see where a natural division occurs in growth habit; this is the juncture where you want to perform the surgery. Put the new plants in pots of soil, and keep them warm and moist for a month while they regain vigor. Then repot them in larger containers of fresh soil, and grow as you would any other fledgling.

quick reference chart

Botanical and Common Name of Vine	Size (inches)	Bloom	Exposure	Remarks
Aeschynanthus lobbianus	36	Spring	Bright	Lush, handsome
A. marmoratus	36	Spring	Bright	Tough to grow
A. speciosus (lipstick vine)	36	Summer	Bright	Fine red flowers
Allamanda nerifolia	60	Spring/ Summer	Sun	Needs space
A. violacea	60	Spring/ Summer	Sun	Dramatic flowers
Antigonon leptotus (queen's wreath)	60	Spring	Sun	Needs training and support
Asparagus sprengeri (emerald fern)	40	*	Bright	Always dependable
Aucuba goldiena (gold dust tree)	40	*	Bright	Large leaves
Begonia 'Elvira Swisher'	40	Fall/ Winter	Bright	Lovely plant
B. 'Gray Feather'	40	Fall/ Winter	Bright	Beautiful foliage
B. 'Orange Rubra'	40	Summer	Bright	Colorful flowers
Bougainvillea 'Barbara Karst'	60	Summer	Sun	Needs plenty of water
B. 'San Diego Red'	60	Summer	Sun	Brilliant red flowers

*Typical foliage plant; not known for flowers.

Botanical and Common Name of Vine	Size (inches)	Bloom	Exposure	Remarks
Brunfelsia calycina floribunda (yesterday-today-and-tomorrow)	48	Winter	Bright	Difficult but worth it
Ceropegia woodii (string-of-hearts)	30	*	Bright	Charming
Cissus antartica (kangaroo ivy)	48	*	Bright/ Shade	Easy-growing vine
C. discolor	40	*	Bright/ Shade	Exquisite foliage
C. rhombifolia (grape ivy)	40	*	Bright/ Shade	Grows fast
Clerodendrum thomsonae (glory bower)	48	Spring/ Summer	Bright	Beautiful flowers
Cobea scandens (cup-and-saucer vine)	30	Summer	Sun	Good seasonal accent
Columnea arguta	36	Spring	Bright	Old favorite
C. 'Butterball'	36	Summer	Bright	Fine yellow flowers
C. microphylla	36	Summer	Bright	Small-leaved beauty
C. 'Yellow Dragon'	36	Summer	Bright	Large flowers
Dipladenia amoena (Mexican love vine)	30	Summer	Sun	One of the best vines
Euphorbia milii (crown-of-thorns)	40	Summer/ Fall	Bright	Overlooked plant
Fatshedera lizei	40	*	Bright/ Shade	Good espalier
Ficus diversifolia (mistletoe fig)	30	*	Bright	Fine branching habit
F. pumila (creeping fig)	40	*	Bright/ Shade	Delightful tiny-leaved creeper
F. radicans variegata	24	*	Bright	Variegated foliage
Geranium (ivy-leaved)	36	Spring/ Summer	Sun	Always handsome

*Typical foliage plant; not known for flowers.

Botanical and Common Name of Vine	Size (inches)	Bloom	Exposure	Remarks
Gloriosa rothschildiana (glory lily)	48	Summer	Sun	Exotic
Hedera helix (ivy)	40	*	Bright	Popular
Hibiscus	48	Fall/ Winter	Sun	Good espalier
Hoya carnosa (wax plant)	36	Summer	Sun/ Bright	Fragrant flowers
Ipomoea 'Heavenly Blue' (morning glory)	48	Summer	Sun	Great seasonal color
I. 'Pearly White' (morning glory)	48	Summer	Sun	Stunning color
Jasminum mesyni (jasmine)	48	Summer	Bright	Good grower
J. nudiflorum (jasmine)	48	Fall	Bright	Lovely fragrance; nonclimbing
J. officinale (jasmine)	48	Summer/ Fall	Bright	Lovely fragrance
J. sambac (jasmine)	48	Summer	Bright	Lovely fragrance
Lantana montevidensis	40	Fall/ Winter	Sun/ Bright	Blooms its head off
Manettia inflata (Mexican firecracker)	24	Winter	Sun	Not spectacular but good
Medinella magnifica (love plant)	40	Summer	Bright	Needs space
Passiflora alato-caerulea (passion flower)	60	Summer	Sun	Exotic flowers
P. edulis (passion flower)	48	Summer	Sun	Old favorite; purple flowers
P. jamesonii (passion flower)	48	Summer	Sun	Old favorite; rose or coral-red flowers
Philodendron andreanum	48	*	Bright/ Shade	Good foliage plant

*Typical foliage plant; not known for flowers.

79

Botanical and Common Name of Vine	Size (inches)	Bloom	Exposure	Remarks
P. 'Burgundy'	40	*	Bright/ Shade	Colorful leaves
P. cordatum	36	*	Bright/ Shade	Popular
P. hastatum	40	*	Bright/ Shade	Arrow-shaped leaves
P. lacinatum	40	*	Bright/ Shade	Good
P. panduraeforme	48	*	Bright/ Shade	Fine performer
P. radiatum	48	*	Bright/ Shade	Decorative
p. variifolium	40	*	Bright/ Shade	Handsome
P. verrucosum	40	*	Bright/ Shade	Exotic
Plectanthus australis (Swedish ivy)	48	*	Bright	Very popular
P. oertendahli (Swedish ivy)	40	*	Bright	Very popular
Plumbago capensis (leadwort)	30	On and off throughout the year	Sun/ Bright	Fast grower
Ruellia amoena	24	Fall/ Winter	Sun/ Bright	Overlooked but good
R. macrantha	24	Fall/ Winter	Sun/ Bright	Overlooked but good
Saxifraga sarmentosa (strawberry begonia)	20	*	Shade	Popular, easy-to-grow plant
S. s. 'Tricolor'	20	*	Bright	Popular easy-to-grow plant
Schizocentron elegans (Spanish shawl)	14	Summer/ Fall	Sun/ Bright	A stellar plant
Scindapsus aureus (pothos)	20	*	Bright	Grows like a weed

*Typical foliage plant; not known for flowers.

Botanical and Common Name of Vine	Size (inches)	Bloom	Exposure	Remarks
S. a. 'Marble Queen' (pothos)	20	*	Bright	Fine, colorful foliage
S. a. 'Silver Moon' (pothos)	20	*	Bright	Fine, colorful foliage
S. pictus argyreus (pothos)	20	*	Bright	Fine, colorful foliage
Stephanotis floribunda (Madagascar jasmine)	26	Summer	Sun/ Bright	Difficult to grow
Syngonium podophyllum (arrowhead plant)	24	*	Bright	Grows quickly
S. p. 'Emerald Gem'	24	*	Bright	Grows quickly
S. p. 'Imperial White'	24	*	Bright	Grows quickly
Thunbergia alata (black-eyed Susan)	*30*	Summer	Sun	Great color
T. erecta (black-eyed Susan)	30	Summer	Sun	Great color
T. grandiflora	30	Fall	Sun	Great color
Tolmiea menziesii (piggyback plant)	30	*	Bright/ Shade	Likes plenty of water
Tradescantia blossfeldiana (wandering Jew)	36	*	Bright	Always good
T. flumensis	36	*	Bright	Always good
T. f. albo-vittata	36	*	Bright	Variegated
T. laekenensis	36	*	Bright	Always good; colorful
T. navicularis	36	*	Bright	Tough to grow
Tropaeolum pentaphyllum (nasturtium)	36	Summer	Sun	One of my favorites
T. speciosum (nasturtium)	40	Summer	Sun	One of my favorites
Vanilla planifolia	48	Summer	Bright	An orchid for indoors
Zebrina pendula	40	*	Bright	Grows fast

*Typical foliage plant; not known for flowers.

Botanical and Common Name of Vine	Size (inches)	Bloom	Exposure	Remarks
Z. p. 'Discolor'	40	*	Bright	Grows fast
Z. p. 'Quadricolor' (wandering Jew)	40	*	Bright	Grows fast

*Typical foliage plant; not known for flowers.

WHERE TO buy plANTS

Orchids and tropical plants	Alberts & Merkel Bros. P.O. Box 537 Boynton Beach, Florida 33435
House plants	W. Atlee Burpee Seed Co. Philadelphia, Pennsylvania 19132 Riverside, California 92502
Large selection of orchids	Margaret Ilgenfritz P.O. Box 665 Monroe, Michigan 48161
House plants of all kinds	Michael J. Kartuz 92 Chestnut Street Wilmington, Massachusetts 91887
Large selection of house plants	Merry Gardens Camden, Maine 04843
House plants	George W. Park Seed Co., Inc. Greenwood, South Carolina 29646
House plants	Tinari Greenhouses 2325 Valley Road Huntington Valley, Pennsylvania 19006